Courage in the Cape:

A Memoir

By Christine Nathan

DEDICATED TO:

My mum and family, whose continual support and encouragement was greatly appreciated.

Rodney Timmerman (17/12/48–14/08/21), Lynda, Talitha, and Dylan, a generous, sacrificial family.

Mark and Jenny Kirby and family: thank you for your commitment to us DTS students.

Rob Vermey (22/10/58–28/08/07), Marianne, Judith, Christian, and Marcia: I valued your companionship and practical help more than words can express!

My buddy and prayer partner Sandra (Butler) Coninck Liefsting, Karel-Jan, and Lailah:
we navigated some confusing, tough times together.

Uncle Ron and Aunty May, wise, kind, gentle treasures in my darkest times.

Elaine Brady, my safety net.

Charles Reed, a young man full of smiles, fun, and friendship who became part of our family. Thank you for all your input with the boys as they adjusted to their new life.

Youth With A Mission staff: Hugh, Melody, and Francois for saying "Yes" to God's call. You're an inspiration.

Thank you for your friendship, generosity, and support that made a significant difference to us as we navigated and adjusted to our new life and mission in South Africa in 1991.

BLESS YOU ALL. WE ARE GRATEFUL.

Contents

Introduction

Part 1: South Africa's history

The people of South Africa

A variety of people groups settled in South Africa over past centuries (through choice or force), leading to its current eclectic population base.

The Bantu, a peaceable farming people, began to migrate from the north into South Africa in AD 250.

In 1488 Portuguese ships arrived at the Cape of Good Hope (Cape Town), looking for fresh supplies. After loading up, they left and didn't return that century. In 1650 the Dutch East India Company established the Dutch Cape Colony, introducing the first Europeans to the country. The Colony's original purpose was to be a small port town for ships travelling to India. Eventually, it became the first white settlement, homing French Huguenot refugees and Dutch and German migrants.

These people called themselves Afrikaners and spoke Afrikaans (also known as Cape Dutch), closely related to the Dutch language.

In 1795 the British occupied the Cape Colony, leading to conflict between the two nations. The British fought the Dutch to gain control. In 1814 the Dutch formally agreed that the colony was part of the British empire.

In 1816 Shaka Zulu formed the Zulu kingdom. This became a mighty nation of fearless, skilled warriors. However, Shaka Zulu was assassinated by his brothers in 1826, and the Zulu empire began to collapse.

The British Parliament abolished slavery in most British colonies in 1833, freeing over 80,000 slaves. William Wilberforce had spearheaded the movement, calling slavery an immoral practice. The government paid twenty million pounds to the slaves' registered owners for the loss of their labour force (business assets). The slaves, however, received no compensation for their brutal, traumatising life of hard work.

From 1835 to 1846 between twelve thousand and fourteen thousand Dutch-speaking colonists left the Cape Colony and travelled to the interior and the east of South Africa. The Boers' migration was called the "Great Trek." Travelling and living in wagons pulled by oxen, the Boers were determined to live somewhere beyond the jurisdiction of the Cape's British colonial administration. Eventually, they formed Boer republics in the Orange Free State and Transvaal.

Britain took over Natal in 1845. At that time, Natal was occupied by British settlers, a few Dutch families, and the local Zulu people. The British allotted over 800,000 hectares to the Zulu people and one million hectares to the white settlers. The rest was called crown land and left untouched.

From 1848 to 1850 labourers were brought from Mauritius to grow and harvest sugar cane. By 1855 several sugar cane mills were flourishing as crops increased. However, local Zulus were not interested in farming white settlers' land, so a cheap labour force was urgently required.

Britain passed a law in 1859 allowing Indian workers to enter and work for five years in return for their passage. Almost 3,500 arrived. Indians were among the most exploited people and received a minimum wage. Those who came as indentured labourers worked and lived under a brutal system close to slavery. From sunrise to sunset, they worked in the agricultural industry as servants, cane workers, cooks, and watchmen, or for the Natal–Transvaal railways as builders. Withholding workers' wages and rations was often used as a punishment. Regardless, when the terms of indenture expired, many stayed on as labourers and farm workers.

The second wave of Indians to arrive were Muslim and Hindu businessmen who paid for their passage. They opened shops and warehouses, with some becoming wealthy. As a result, Durban became home to the largest group of Indians living outside India. They made a significant contribution to South Africa's economy and culture.

The coloured or mixed-race community was the second-largest group of non-whites. It included Indians, Malays, and descendants of native Africans, all of whom had had children to the early white settlers. Eighty-nine percent of coloured people lived in the Cape colony. Like the Indians, coloureds were neither black nor white. They were in the middle of the colour classification. Their unclear status sometimes generated fears of being reduced to the level of the blacks.

The Khoisan people of the Cape were hunter-gatherers who married Dutch sailors in the 17th century. Their children were the ancestors of the Xhosa people. The Xhosa were peaceful people who raised cattle. They lived in the Cape region, Botswana, and Namibia.

Malays were taken to South Africa as slaves in the 18th century. They were skilled artisans who built beautiful furniture decorated with ornate engravings.

The quest for power

In 1856 the Boers of Transvaal declared their territory a republic. A decade later, in 1866, diamonds were discovered at Kimberley, located between the Vaal and Orange rivers. Gold was also discovered in 1866, leading to an enormous gold rush. The city of Johannesburg in the Transvaal expanded rapidly from the influx of gold diggers. In 1877 Transvaal was taken by the British.

The British wanted all of South Africa united as a single British confederation. Because they were concerned at the increasing numbers of firearms possessed by the Zulus, the British army commander sent an injunction to the Zulu King, Cetshwayo, in December 1878, directing him to disband his army. Knowing it would mean a loss of power, Cetshwayo refused.

Early in 1879 the British invaded with 15,000 soldiers who had superior military technology. In response, a large Zulu force of 25,000 warriors made a surprise attack and defeated the British, who quickly vacated the Zulu Kingdom. Meanwhile, fierce fighting continued in other places. As a result, Britain sent out more troops and artillery. However, the Zulu forces continued to win battles, including attacking a supply convoy.

In June 1879 Cetshwayo tried to strike a peace deal, but Lord Chelmsford, still smarting from the initial defeat, refused. Chelmsford was about to resign and intended to end his career in a blaze of glory. Once fresh troops and artillery arrived from Britain, a final battle began at Ulundi. The decisive defeat of the Zulus left them decimated, enabling the British to control Zululand. Four weeks later, Lord Chelmsford resigned. In August 1879 Cetshwayo was captured and sent into exile in Cape Town, then London.

On December 16, 1880, the First Boer War began between the Boers and the British. The Boers won, gaining independence for Transvaal and the Orange Free State.

The Second Boer War (also known as the Anglo-Boer War) began on October 11, 1889. Britain wanted control of the Boers' two lucrative independent states, the South African Republic and the Orange Free State. The British won the war on May 31, 1902, and claimed the two rogue states.

Key events leading to apartheid

1893   Mohandas (Mahātmā) Gandhi, a pacifist Indian lawyer, arrived in South Africa. He played an integral role in South Africa's political transformation.

1894 Gandhi formed South Africa's first Indian political organisation (NIC).

1910   The four colonies and republics (Cape Colony, Natal, Transvaal, and Orange Free State) became the "Union of South Africa."

1912   African activists formed the African National Congress (ANC).

1913   The Natives Land Act imposed segregation of land based on race.

1914   Afrikaans was adopted for use and became a compulsory language in schools.

1917 onwards: many Indian ex-labourers remained, flourished in commercial enterprises, and became landowners on Durban's east coast.

1919   Afrikaans was adopted in the Dutch Reformed Church. Jan Smuts became the first elected prime minister of South Africa.

1930   All whites over the age of twenty-one, including women, were guaranteed the right to vote.

1930   South Africa declared independence from the United Kingdom.

1936   The Indian population was now 219,925. Half had been born in South Africa.

1939   World War II began. South Africa served as a valuable seaport for the allies.

1961 South Africa declared itself a republic (an independent nation). The government divided the 37 million residents into four official groups: Africans (blacks), about 75 percent (of whom 45 percent were under the age of fifteen); whites, 13 percent; coloured, 9 percent; and Indians, 3 percent. Black and white people led separate lives with few points of contact.

Apartheid system enforced

In 1948 the white National Government was voted into power, with Hendrik Verwoerd as President. Verwoerd was a politician who had studied psychology and sociology and was the editor of an Afrikaner newspaper. He was regarded as the architect of apartheid.

The Population Registration Act was the cornerstone of the apartheid policy that legalised discrimination. It was introduced in 1950 and divided South Africans into four broad groups based on skin colour and ethnicity (white, black, Indian, and coloured), enforcing the minority government's policy of racial segregation. Bold signs were erected throughout the nation, designating which shops, beaches, restaurants, theatres, or even outdoor benches each group could use.

Homelands with rudimentary schools and hospitals were created for blacks, who were denied voting rights. The Pass Laws were initiated to control the movement of "native men" in both South Africa and Zimbabwe. Male teenagers and adults were required to register at the Pass Office to obtain a certificate, which they had to carry while travelling from one district to another and when seeking employment. Their movements were restricted and tightly controlled.

Black African men provided a cheap source of able-bodied labourers, maximising profits for their white bosses. However, they were excluded from the manufacturing sector and limited to working for a pittance. In 1959 the laws were changed so black Africans could bargain for a decent wage. This led to powerful African trade unions being established in 1962 for textiles, railways, tailoring, and municipalities workers. Unfortunately, soon after a law was passed making it an offence for workers in any essential service industry to strike.

The policy of racial segregation favoured the political and economic power of the white minority. This disastrous policy impacted South Africa and continues to do so today. The segregation laws were invasive and complete; it was even a criminal offence for a non-white person to marry or have sexual relations with a white person. If discovered, the non-white offender (but not the white offender) would be prosecuted.

Forced removals, where the army rounded up non-whites and took them to specific areas away from the central city or town to live, created an enormous upheaval countrywide. Close-knit communities were destroyed, and children had to attend schools in their new area. It was traumatic for all the non-whites (and a few whites) who were relocated if their homes were in a newly designated non-white area. By emphasising the differences among the various ethnic groups, the government turned the four groups against each other.

Education

When the apartheid government came to power in 1948, it saw the schooling system as the primary vehicle for propagating its beliefs. In 1953 Dr. Hendrik Verwoerd introduced the Bantu [black South African] Education Act to Parliament. He said, "I want to remind the Honourable Members of Parliament that if the native in South Africa has been taught to expect that he will lead his adult life under the policy of equal rights, he is making a big mistake. The native must not be subject to a school system which draws him away from his own community and misleads him by showing him the green pastures of European society in which he's not allowed to graze." This marked the tone of the apartheid education system from 1959 onwards.

Apart from a few mixed private schools, there were separate schools for the four population groups. It was illegal for a student to attend any state school designated for another group. Schools could not educate someone from a different group. There were glaring inequalities between the four schooling systems, including teacher qualifications, teacher-pupil ratios, per capita funding, buildings, equipment, facilities, books, stationery, and the results measured in the proportions and levels of certificates awarded. Nineteen education departments were established, with each designated ethnic group having a separate infrastructure that the government tightly controlled.

White schools were heavily funded, while Indian and coloured schools received less. Black schools received insufficient buildings and equipment, untrained teachers, and limited funding. Schooling was compulsory for whites, Indians, and coloureds, but not for blacks.

Timeline of Nelson Mandela

Nelson (birth name Rolihlahla) Mandela was born July 18, 1918, into the Madiba clan. His father was Nkosi

Mandela, principal counsellor to the Acting King of the Thembu people. The white government summoned Nkosi to appear in court. When he refused, they stripped him of his title, land, and cattle.

Rolihlahla's mother took him to her small village, where missionaries ran a Christian school. He lived in a small hut and took care of cattle and sheep. His father visited them until he became ill. After his father's death, Nelson became part of King Jongintaba's family and lived in a large modern home. The king drove a car and wore European suits. As a child, Nelson attended tribal meetings. His foster father did not speak until he had listened to everyone's opinion first. Nelson learnt from his example.

An elder explained the blacks' plight as marginalised people in a short story. "When the Europeans came to South Africa, they had the Bible, and we had the land. When they said, "Let us pray," we closed our eyes. When we opened them, we had the Bible while they had the land!" Nelson dreamed of making his own contribution to the freedom struggle of his people. He longed to be a leader, governing his land with justice and equality.

At primary school in Qunu, his teacher gave him the name Nelson as it was customary to give schoolchildren a "Christian" name. Nelson later went to boarding school, then Fort Hare College (the only all-black college) to prepare for his future as a leader. Nelson studied other countries' cultures, economies, and political systems.

In 1940 Nelson protested against the meagre meals and conditions at the college and was expelled. The king ordered him to return to college, but he refused and ran away to Johannesburg. After talking with the king, Nelson was allowed to begin law studies.

Nelson joined the African National Congress (ANC) party in 1944, marrying his first wife, Evelyn Mase, the same year. Their oldest son was born the following year.

In 1948 apartheid laws were passed in parliament. Black Africans had no power or voice in their land and were denied the vote. Since his younger years, Nelson had longed to see all people equal and free to choose their own destiny.

Nelson was elected President of the ANC in 1950. Two years later, Oliver Tambo and Nelson opened the first law firm representing black people. They sent a letter to the government stating that black people would refuse to comply with the apartheid laws from February 29, 1952, if the apartheid laws were not abolished. The ANC's complaints were rejected, and they were threatened with severe punishment. Many people were beaten, arrested, and fined. Oliver and Nelson launched the Defiance Campaign in June 1952, which included peaceful protests such as sitting on "whites only" beaches.

Nelson travelled extensively, encouraging blacks to fight for their rights with courage and to control their anger after years of oppression. Their goal was to end unjust laws.

The inspiration for passive resistance was an effective strategy that Mahatma Gandhi, an Indian lawyer, and Martin Luther King Jnr. from the United States had both used to gain equal rights for their people. This powerful strategy had turned public opinion away from oppression in both nations.

Nations worldwide watched the ANC's courage while the South African government openly used violence. Police raided homes, arresting, torturing, and killing black leaders. Nelson, labelled a troublemaker by the government, was forbidden to travel beyond his neighbourhood, join groups, or write articles. Sadly, passive resistance failed, and many blacks died while protesting.

Missionary schools were banned in 1953, and a new education law was passed that prepared the "inferior" blacks to serve the whites.

In 1956 Nelson (aged thirty-eight) and the ANC leadership were arrested and tried for treason. The trial dragged on till 1961, during which time they lived at home on bail. Nelson's wife divorced him in 1958, and he met and married Winnie. Their first daughter, Zenani, was born the following year. Finally, in 1959, 126 of the ANC leaders were released. Thirty of the leaders, however, including Nelson, still faced charges.

An anti-apartheid demonstration in 1960 at the black township of Sharpeville turned into a massacre. White police shot sixty-nine black residents. Thirty-one women and nineteen children were killed by bullets in their backs as they fled, and a further 180 residents were severely injured. The South African government dismissed the international outcry. As a result, investors pulled out of South Africa. A state of emergency was declared, and all public meetings banned. The ANC leadership sent their representative Oliver Tambo outside South Africa for his safety. He visited many nations calling for support for the oppressed peoples of South Africa.

In 1961 all treason charges were dropped due to lack of proof. Nelson and the other leaders were released. Nelson went underground, meeting with reporters secretly. Nelson had previously advocated non-violent protests, but after Sharpeville, his beliefs changed. A new group, called "Umkhonto we Sizwe" (The Spear of the Nation), was formed. Its goal was armed resistance and sabotage without violence.

Nelson was arrested in 1962 and sentenced to five years of hard labour. The following year saw him on trial, facing a death sentence. For five months, Nelson listened to accusations. His reply was, "We believe that South Africa belongs to all people who live in it and not to any one group, be it black or white." Nelson addressed the hardships and injustices imposed by the government eloquently and passionately, ending by declaring, "I have dedicated myself to this struggle of the African people. It is an ideal which I hope to live for and achieve. But if needs be, it is an ideal for which I am prepared to die."

Nelson and the ANC leaders were sentenced to life imprisonment at Robben Island in 1964. The conditions were harsh; there were no beds and they spent all day breaking rocks. For eighteen years, Nelson lived in an eight- by seven-foot cell, with the lightbulb shining day and night. He slept on a thin mattress with old, worn-out blankets, even on icy cold winter nights. His toilet was a bucket. Nelson only received two letters a year; both were heavily edited. He didn't see his wife or children for many years, and his eyes became damaged because of the sun's bright reflection on the limestone he broke into pieces for so long. Nelson exercised each day and studied law, Afrikaner history, and languages in the evenings. He encouraged the other prisoners to study. While ill, he was kept in a solitary wet, cold cell and given only rice and water. Oliver Tambo spoke to leaders and the press in different nations about Nelson's plight and the injustices of apartheid. Foreign leaders called for Nelson's release.

Nelson's wife, Winnie, was also arrested and kept in solitary confinement for fifteen months, during which time their girls were without both parents. Winnie became a bitter, aggressive freedom fighter upon her release.

In 1976 a law was passed forcing all students to study in Afrikaans. As this was a foreign language to most black students, it would hinder their education. In Soweto, many thousands of school children protested peacefully. However, one thousand young children and teens were shot and killed by the police. Not one policeman was injured.

Nelson was offered a reduced sentence in exchange for supporting a "Homelands" system where blacks were forcibly removed to live in designated areas. They would not be South African citizens and would need work permits to enter white towns and cities. Nelson refused to be part of this apartheid scheme.

In 1977 activist Steve Biko was tortured by police, then chained to a wall where he died. Again, there was a horrified international outcry. Twelve western nations sent representatives to pay their respects at his funeral, while renewed calls for trade sanctions increased.

Nelson was seen as the leader of the oppressed peoples of South Africa and a symbol of hope. Riots became common as people demanded his release. Finally, the government made some concessions: blacks were allowed to use all buses and attend all theatres, and electricity was made available in some townships. Coloured and Indian people were allowed to elect their own representatives for the government.

Nelson was taken to Pollsmoor Prison in Cape Town in 1982. After two decades of sleeping on a cold concrete floor, he finally had a bed. At last, he saw his two daughters.

In 1989 F. W. de Klerk was elected president of South Africa. He began negotiating with Nelson, who stated, "Only free men can negotiate. Prisoners cannot enter into contracts. Your freedom and mine cannot be separated." In 1990 de Klerk removed the ban on the ANC party, and Nelson, aged seventy-one, was released from prison. Fifty thousand people waited outside Cape Town City Hall to hear their future leader.

Nelson travelled in South Africa and internationally, preaching forgiveness and an end to police and government violence. He held onto his dream of a united nation where everyone worked together peacefully, continuing to demand a vote for every person. "When I was sent to prison twenty-seven years ago, I had no vote. When I came out, I still had no vote. That is due to the colour of my skin!"

In August 1992 (when the boys and I were living in South Africa), the ANC called for a nationwide general strike as there had been no changes. Millions of non-whites stayed home to protest their hatred of apartheid. During a September rally, soldiers killed twenty-nine ANC members and injured two hundred more.

On September 26, 1992, President de Klerk and Nelson signed "A Record of Understanding," a commitment to find agreement on the governance of South Africa. Nelson said, "Your mind must dominate your emotions so you can work towards a harmonious society with your former enemies who put you into prison for twenty-seven years!" The Nobel Peace Prize was awarded to Nelson Mandela and F. W. de Klerk in 1993.

The first democratic elections, with 40 million people eligible to vote, were held in 1994. Nelson Mandela was elected the first black president of South Africa, with F. W. de Klerk serving as his deputy president. Extreme widespread poverty was a huge problem; Nelson donated a significant portion of his salary to children in need.

In 1996 Nelson divorced his militant wife, Winnie, and in 1997 withdrew from national politics. He married Grace Machel, a children's rights activist from Mozambique, in 1998. Nelson was eighty.

Thabo Mbeki was elected President of South Africa in 1999. In 2005 one of Nelson's sons died of AIDS. Nelson devoted himself to promoting education about Aids.

Nelson Rolihlahla Mandela died on December 5, 2013. The world mourned a gentle freedom fighter, recognised locally and internationally as a man of peace and wisdom.

Part 2: Bridging—Ignorance about South Africa

In 1990, before the advent of the internet and Google, I searched for information to prepare us for our move to South Africa. Unfortunately, in our small town in New Zealand, the only source of accessible information was the local library. There was one book on South Africa, a glossy-covered promotional book that focused on industry, mining, and the positive aspects of life in South Africa. In reality, the book was selective and sanitised, failing to mention the infamous squatter settlements, coloured and black townships, or any reference to segregation. Rather, it was created to persuade potential tourists and the international community that South Africa was a prosperous, harmonious nation. Naturally, this biased and misleading book did not prepare us in any way for the realities we would face.

New Zealand's culture was more inclusive. We were a curious nation with a strong sense of justice. Our response to the injustices we heard about and saw on television was to boycott the Springboks from playing on New Zealand soil. The New Zealand government restricted our national rugby team, the "All Blacks," from playing in South Africa. The television occasionally showed glimpses of desperate people living in squalor and poverty, but as I had not expected to live in South Africa, I hadn't taken much notice. However, when I met John Dawson in 1990, and he advised me to do my missions training in South Africa, I realised I needed to familiarise myself with the political situation there. That was only a few months before we left New Zealand; as a result, I was ignorant about what we would encounter.

January 1991, when we arrived in South Africa, was a time of great political unrest as well as a historic and exciting time to be living there. President F. W. de Klerk was abolishing the apartheid laws and preparing to give the black population the vote for the first time in the nation's history. Nelson Mandela had just been released from prison, bringing hope to the long-suffering non-whites that their plight was about to change drastically. De Klerk faced hostility and opposition from his own party, but as a Christian man he knew apartheid had to end. I admired him greatly for his courage and tenacity.

Naturally, Nelson's release aroused very strong reactions from all the different groups. Thousands of white people were hurriedly applying to immigrate to Britain, Canada, New Zealand, or Australia to avoid what they believed would be a bloodbath when Nelson Mandela and his ANC party came to power.

Some of these people were Rhodesian citizens who had fled their country only ten years before, in 1980, when Robert Mugabe became the first black president of Rhodesia (which he renamed Zimbabwe). They had assumed there would be retribution for the decades of subjugation and injustice towards the black population in Zimbabwe. However, it was a peaceful transition, and the incoming government blended the white and non-white armies and other government departments. After establishing a new life in South Africa, the ex-Rhodesian folk were now experiencing the same dilemma of uncertainty for their families' safety, education, and future employment opportunities.

These were turbulent, intense, and uncertain times for the South African population of over 40 million people.

Life, as everyone had known it for many decades, was about to change radically, and no one knew what the outcome would be of having an inexperienced black government leading the nation.

White people who had enjoyed incredibly privileged lives with the assurance of employment, a home, good education, and servants had the most to lose. The disadvantaged black majority, who often lived in squalor due to unemployment rates of up to 80 percent in some townships, had sudden high expectations of improved living conditions. Many adults scrambled daily to find work, standing at street corners waiting for a white man to drive by and offer them temporary work.

During the forced removal era, soldiers had driven the blacks to remote, barren areas where they had to walk long distances each day to catch buses or trains to reach their places of employment. This constant stress of hoping to earn enough money to buy food and paraffin to cook with took its toll on their health. Instead of sporadically earning a pittance, they now hoped for a reversal of their desperate way of life.

Sadly, most black people still had no running water, electricity, or toilets in the informal settlements where they lived. Even when employed as miners, cleaners, maids, or gardeners, their family's education, living conditions, and health care was often inadequate.

The boys and I arrived into this turbulent, unsettled country with little knowledge or understanding of the multi-layered, complex society we were entering.

Left: Joshua, me, and Eli, December 1990.

Below: With family and friends at Auckland airport — leaving NZ.

Foreword

My first book, *Journey to Courage,* tells the story of single mother Christine Nathan's many challenges, including an abusive marriage and a deep sense of not belonging anywhere. At the age of twenty-seven, Christine became a Christian and began a lifetime journey of healing, restoration, and acquiring much-needed wisdom about God and life.

God revealed to Christine that He had work for her to do in Zimbabwe, Africa. In late 1990 she sold her home and flew to Africa with her two sons, sixteen-year-old Joshua and ten-year-old Eli. Initially, all three travelled to Sydney. From there, Eli flew straight to Zimbabwe to holiday with his father and family, while Christine and Joshua journeyed to London, France, Belgium, Holland, and Nairobi before landing in Cape Town. Eli joined them a few days later.

The boys began schooling in a historical era when the "white" schools opened up to children of all four racial groups for the first time since the apartheid regime began. Christine began her missions training by attending a Discipleship Training School (DTS) at Youth With A Mission (YWAM) in Muizenberg. The DTS would prepare her to serve in disadvantaged communities, especially among widows and orphans.

In book two, join Christine and the boys as they enter South Africa during the apartheid era, just as Nelson Mandela is released after twenty-seven years in prison. With little knowledge of South Africa or the apartheid system, they are naive and entirely unprepared for what they encounter upon their arrival. It is immediately evident their new country is steeped in discriminatory laws that had created deep pain and anger following decades of racism. The difference between South Africa and their own laid-back New Zealand culture is enormous.

Author's note:

In this book, I will be using the standard terms used by the people of South Africa to describe themselves and other cultures. During apartheid, everyone was classified into four racial groups: white, black, Indian, or coloured/mixed-race. As a New Zealander who had never referred to anyone by the colour of their skin, I found this system of identification offensive and hard to use. However, I will use these terms for accuracy in relating my adventures in South Africa.

THE TOWN OF CONISTON IS FICTIONAL, ALTHOUGH IT

REPRESENTS A REAL PLACE. SOME NAMES HAVE BEEN CHANGED

TO PROTECT PRIVACY.

CHAPTER 1

Muizenberg

After a long flight from London via Nairobi, Josh and I landed in Cape Town to begin our new life. Eli was still in Zimbabwe but would arrive in two days. To my delight, as we came through customs and into the arrival hall, I saw two men with a YWAM sign waiting for us. I was so relieved and excited that I gave them both a big hug and a kiss on the cheek, which I later learnt had startled them.

Culturally, South Africans were more reserved with strangers, so they put my enthusiasm down to probably being typical of a New Zealand greeting! Not so. It was simply sheer relief that we had finally made it to Africa after ten years of waiting and facing many daunting challenges along the way. The two men introduced themselves as Dave and Rodney, staff members of the Discipleship Training School (DTS) I would be attending.

After loading our luggage into a van, Dave and Rodney drove us along a modern highway, passing some of the most beautiful and stately homes I had ever seen. Our traditional homes in New Zealand were smaller, with three or four bedrooms, surrounded by lawns and gardens. These homes we drove past were set against a magnificent backdrop of huge mountains and were several times larger than what I was used to. The gardens looked like something out of a Homes and Gardens magazine, perfectly manicured by black gardeners who were working on most of the properties, clipping hedges, planting flowers, and mowing lawns. Black maids dressed in pastel floral uniforms with matching caps were numerous, and some had a white baby or toddler tied to their back with a wide strip of coloured cloth. Other maids were standing on street corners with a baby on their back or holding a white child's hand while they chatted. I was surprised to see how obediently the children stood next to the maids in the hot sun. Watching the servants working on the properties was a surprise. In New Zealand, most people took care of their own homes, lawns, and gardens.

The highways were in excellent condition, making for an enjoyable ride. However, it was strange to be driving through expensive European suburbs with names such as Bishops Court and Constantia. I had expected to encounter a more typical African environment similar to what I had seen on television documentaries and travel programmes. Processing the passing scenery made me realise I was pretty ignorant about the impact of the apartheid system, which had segregated the different cultures into separate areas. At this stage I was not aware that the impoverished townships were usually located far from the main highways, so our first impression of South Africa was very skewed.

In contrast, several beggars and vendors stood near the traffic lights waiting for vehicles to stop. The vendors sold various wares, including food, clothing, and kitchenware, which they dangled in front of the car windows, calling out a price for each item. While we waited for the lights to turn green, the beggars offered to clean the front windows quickly or take the car rubbish away for a small fee. This was the first time in my life I had encountered anyone begging for a few cents. Dressed in old, dirty, or ragged clothing, they looked defeated and downtrodden. Finally, after about thirty minutes of driving past various densely populated middle-class suburbs with names like Claremont, Rosebank, Mowbray, and Plumstead, we arrived at Muizenberg, a small seaside town.

The two features that immediately stood out were a beautiful long beach with white sand and a majestic mountain that rose just behind the main road. The town lay at the foot of the mountain, with homes hugging the gentle lower slopes. The main road ran between the houses and a railway line situated close to the edge of the winding coastline. Surprisingly, the tracks seemed to sit on top of the large rocks. I looked forward to taking a ride to all the other little villages and towns around False Bay. I could see that Muizenberg had looked stunning in its heyday, with many large hotels by the shoreline, but it now appeared as a tired, slightly shabby holiday town.

Muizenberg and coastal villages.

Rodney parked the van near a two-storey hotel called Surf Inn, which YWAM had purchased the year before. This would be our living quarters for the next three months.

On the first floor, Rodney showed me into a narrow room that had one small wardrobe and a set of bunks for myself and my roommate, Judy, to share. Rodney told me that Judy, a twenty-six-year-old physiotherapist, was deaf, so I would need to make sure I looked at her when speaking and not speak fast. I knew this would be a challenge for me, as New Zealanders typically speak fast. Also, since we would be sleeping on bunks—her on the top bunk and me below— I realized there wouldn't be much chatting once we were in bed, because we couldn't

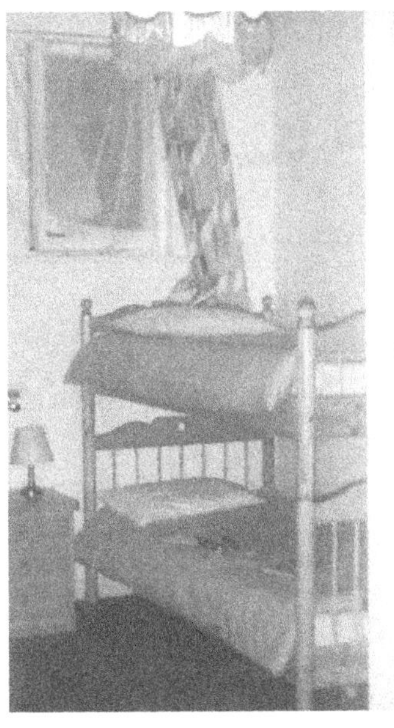

My tiny room.

see each other's face in the dark! Nevertheless, I admired Judy for attending the course and wondered how she would cope with the lectures. Lying on the dresser was a "welcome basket" filled with goodies and a card. When I commented to one of the staff about the chunk of stale bread in the basket, he laughed and informed me it was a treat called a rusk. The best way to enjoy it was to dunk it in hot tea or coffee. I later learnt to appreciate the delicious taste of the buttermilk rusks I had initially rejected.

The boys' bedroom was next to mine, with an adjoining door. Their room was larger, with a front view of the train tracks, the road, and the imposing mountain. They also had bunk beds and one desk for homework. A communal lounge was right outside both our rooms. I was glad the boys would be sleeping close by, but I was concerned they wouldn't be free to pop in whenever they wanted to talk, because I was sharing a room with another lady. After unpacking our clothes and some essentials, I wandered around the first floor to see who else had arrived. We were a few days early, so there weren't many students yet. As I looked in the other rooms, I noticed that all the furniture was pine, which went with the beachy vibe of the hotel.

The first person I met was a young staff member who had recently finished her Discipleship School. She was friendly and open but then surprised me by sharing a problem she was having with her boyfriend. Being twice her age, I unexpectedly became an instant mother figure to her. At this point, I realised I needed to adjust my expectations of the school staff, who I had assumed would all be mature, seasoned missionaries.

As the school hadn't started yet, Josh and I went outside to investigate our new surroundings. We both loved the idea of living by the sea. I had grown up near a beach, and Josh (17) was anticipating many afternoons and weekends surfing with the other students. He was a friendly lad, so I knew he would thrive among the young students. I looked forward to Eli (10) joining us

Muizenberg beach.

and watching his reaction when he discovered we lived in a two-storey hotel near the beach. His holiday in Zimbabwe had been a significant time for Eli, as he hadn't stayed with his father or met his younger siblings before.

When Josh and I walked along the beach we saw several brightly coloured huts similar to those on British beaches. They seemed incongruous in an African setting; I hadn't yet realised the extent to which colonialists imprinted their own culture on "conquered" nations. The white sand was smooth, with tourists reclining on deck chairs and towels while enjoying the brilliant sunshine and inviting blue sea. Warm, shallow waters provided an ideal place for little children to play, while the waves offered keen surfers hours of sport. National and international surfers were drawn to Muizenberg by some of the best surfing conditions in South Africa.

Making our way up the main road, Josh and I passed an old shop with the delicious aroma of freshly baked bread wafting out the door. The owners were Portuguese and had recently begun supplying YWAM with crates of hot bread every day. Further up the road, we walked under a railway bridge to a new shopping centre where a supermarket, bank, and book shop was located. I felt overwhelmed in the supermarket as none of the labels or brands were familiar. Which fruit juice would be tasty, and which wouldn't? This was a mammoth exercise in trial and error.

Over the next three months, we discovered that the overhead railway bridge was actually quite a hazard to unsuspecting truck drivers. On several occasions we heard a huge bang nearby and rushed outside to look for the source. Each time, we saw a large truck jammed under the bridge. The top of the front cab, which had borne the brunt of the collision, looked like a concertina. Usually, a disorientated driver was staggering around scratching his head. Unfortunately, the driver hadn't noticed a sign warning truck drivers about the clearance height needed to pass under the bridge. The result was a crushed roof, bruised bodies, and a great deal of stress for the driver, who had to explain to his boss that the expensive truck was severely damaged. After the truck's tyres were deflated, the vehicle could be towed out from under the tracks. I invariably felt sorry for the drivers.

Muizenberg was a typical little beach town with a diverse population that included a small community of elderly Jewish people, many English-speaking families, and some Afrikaner and English retirees. An interesting collection of informal dwellers, including some hippy types and homeless people who were partial to alcohol, had set up home in the bush nearby. Refugees from the Congo, Rwanda, and other nations inhabited sprawling old buildings that landlords rented out cheaply by the room. Occasionally a group of keen young surfers would arrive for the season, adding to the multi-faceted population.

The domestic servants who lived in small rooms at the back of their employers' homes were a less visible group. They were not allowed to use the facilities inside their employers' homes so shared an outside toilet and tap with other servants.

The newly-arrived YWAM staff added more nationalities, as did the international students who flew in every three months.

Each South African ethnic group had its own distinct role. White people typically owned or ran most businesses and operated the tills, while black people had the more menial roles of cleaning in restaurants and working as domestic servants and labourers. They even raked the sand on the beach daily, keeping it in pristine condition for the local white population and the many tourists to enjoy.

Black people were forbidden by law from visiting and enjoying these same beaches. I couldn't believe my eyes one morning when I saw a middle-aged African man with a rake methodically smoothing out the sand. I wondered what he must think about making this place so beautiful for foreigners while he and his family would never enjoy the fruits of his labour. This injustice was one of many that resulted from the harsh apartheid laws that had elevated white people to a privileged position. Many groups were oppressed and restricted just because of their skin colour. At times it took my breath away to see the negative impact these racially inspired laws had on the millions of non-whites who made up the majority of the South African population.

Surf Inn.

CHAPTER 2

Surf Inn

Back at Surf Inn, Josh set off to find some students his own age while I helped the young staff make up bunk beds for incoming students.

My school leader and his wife, Mark and Jenny Kirby, came to introduce themselves. Mark was excited about leading the DTS, while Jenny would take care of their young child and help out in practical ways. She was a bubbly, friendly person who offered to help me shop for the lads' school uniforms and supplies. I was grateful for this, as I didn't know where to go or how much any of it would cost. The Kirbys told me the cost of living was low compared to New Zealand. However, inflation had hit recently, and prices were now increasing significantly. This meant I would need to handle our remaining money very carefully.

Mark explained that I was the oldest student, and we were the only family attending the DTS. This didn't bother me. I loved meeting strangers, and after many years of bringing up the boys and running a home on my own, community life was very appealing. I looked forward to the companionship and fun I hoped would be part of our life at Surf Inn. Mark told me to take off any time I needed, stating, "It's God first, family second, and the course third." I appreciated his concern for us.

Each day, eager students arrived from around the world. It was an exciting time getting to know each other and sharing our stories of how we had ended up in Muizenberg at YWAM. For most of us, this was our first time in South Africa, so everything was new and fascinating. I quickly bonded with a cockney girl from London named Polly, and also Sandra, a young local lady from the Cape region.

Sandra was beautiful, with a uniquely colourful and feminine way of dressing. Her dark hair was long, thick, and curly. A gorgeous smile and great sense of humour added to her appeal. Sandra was part of a group that the government had labelled coloured/mixed-race. She was well-educated, dignified, confident, and resourceful, and I admired her. We bonded the first day we met and are still close friends thirty years later.

It was exciting for Polly and me to discover how cheap watermelons and boxes of grapes were in the local supermarket. These fruits were a luxury item in our own countries, but here they only cost ten rand (R 10, the equivalent of NZ$1) for a whole watermelon or a box of light green Hanepoot grapes. We returned to Surf Inn laden with fresh fruit and huge smiles on our faces, eager to taste the delicious, sweet grapes.

I was happy that some things were cheap, as outfitting the lads for their school uniforms had cost NZ$1000. Gulp. My remaining money was dwindling by the day.

Later that afternoon, Eli arrived from Zimbabwe with his massive bag of Lego. For days, when I looked into the boys' bedroom, I saw several young guys lounging on the floor, engrossed in creating all sorts of Lego vehicles and buildings. Eli was initially unhappy that students kept invading his private space, but he soon adjusted and became friends with the older lads.

Boys' room with Lego.

Josh and I enjoyed hearing about Eli's time with his dad, Joyce (his dad's gentle, kind wife), and his two younger siblings. The dynamics Eli encountered in his father's home were very different to our family, where there was no father figure and Eli was the youngest sibling. Suddenly he had the role of being an older brother in Zimbabwe, with a dad who had a flourishing engineering company, a personal driver, and servants in the family home. The small city they lived in was limited in activities, so Eli spent much of his time playing with his siblings and taking dozens of photos of monkeys frolicking among the trees in the back garden.

Eli with his siblings.

My first priority was to buy the boys' school uniforms and supplies, then enrol them into their schools before my lectures began. Jenny took Eli and me to meet the headmaster at Muizenberg Junior School, which had 250 pupils. He was a friendly Christian who informed us that, as Afrikaans was a compulsory subject, Eli would have a lot of catching up to do. The headmaster arranged for language tapes so Eli could practise at home. Thankfully, some of the Afrikaner students on base also offered to tutor Eli, who was unaware that he was the first "coloured" child many of these students had related to in such a close way.

His attendance at the junior school was part of a historic milestone in South African history. Local schools were opening their doors to non-white students for the first time in decades because the white parents and staff had recently voted against separatism. Previously, all children attended schools in specific geographic areas based on the four official categories of black, coloured, white, or Indian.

Eli and younger brother Tawanda.

To my relief, neither of my lads experienced this racial segregation, but if we had come to South Africa the year before, they would not have been allowed to attend the local schools. Once again, I saw God's wisdom in delaying the selling of our home. This January DTS was the perfect timing for my boys in ways we hadn't realized when we were back home in the South Pacific, impatiently waiting for our house to sell.

One of the students observed that Josh was like a cat enjoying a big bowl of cream. He looked so happy living in a community with many young people. An obvious bonus was that he had musicians to jam with and several surfers to spend time with. In addition, groups of students regularly set up volleyball games at the beach. The boys enjoyed all these activities.

Josh and Charlie.

Josh's school, Muizenberg High, presented a massive challenge for him. He would be in Standard 10, the final year of secondary education and would have to sit the national exam, Matric. One of the compulsory subjects to pass was Afrikaans, a language Josh had never heard of before. I felt concerned for him with this daunting task before him. Thankfully, he had an optimistic nature and enjoyed new challenges, so he soon learnt different greetings and essential phrases.

Being a friendly extrovert, Josh made many new friends and was popular among the younger students at YWAM, some of whom were only a year older than him.

Eli's buddy Ryan.

CHAPTER 3

Orientation

Forty-seven eager students from New Zealand, England, Denmark, Ghana, Germany, Switzerland, and South Africa gathered on the morning of Monday, 14 January 1991 to begin the much-anticipated Discipleship Training School (DTS).

We sat around tables in small groups, eagerly waiting for our leader and his team to introduce themselves. We were keen to know who they were and what had drawn them to YWAM. After greeting us, Mark introduced himself and proceeded to give us an overview of the history of YWAM South Africa.

Mark had joined the army aged seventeen, then trained for four years as an aircraft instrument technician. After working for two years, he joined YWAM in Delmas, where he met his future wife, Jenny. They married in 1987. The Delmas base was an isolated rented rural property in the north of South Africa, twenty-five kilometres from the nearest town. About twenty families and several single staff members lived in a communal setting.

Mark and Jenny Kirby.

In 1989 Mark led his first DTS. Soon after, the Lord began speaking to the leadership of the base, revealing that it was a new season. YWAM would own their next property and would not rent again. The staff were asked to pray and seek God for the new location. Mark and several others felt that Cape Town was their next destination. He was keen to move there, as God had revealed to him as a child that he would live there one day.

Five of the base leadership team travelled to Cape Town to spy out the land. The Lord directed them to the small seaside town of Muizenberg and supplied enough finance to purchase three large properties. The first was a two-storey hotel with many bedrooms, called Surf Inn. It was perfect for running training schools and accommodating large numbers of students. One of the rooms would be set aside for guests, particularly family members who wanted to check out their son or daughter's new environment. Hospitality was an essential part of YWAM's culture and values.

The second property was an older two-storey house in Cromer Road, which had enough rooms for reception, administration, finance, and the registrar's office. The third property was a block of self-contained flats near Surf Inn. These units were ideal for second-level students attending a twelve-month course called the School of Biblical Studies (SBS), which required a quiet environment for the many hours of study. Around August 1989 the staff began moving to the Cape region, where the families and singles searched for affordable accommodation.

Mark later shared some background information about the base's history with me, giving me some interesting insights into what was happening before our arrival. In 1990 as the staff settled into rental homes and flats in and around Muizenberg, a new season of pioneering and establishing a YWAM community began. Because everyone was now living in varied locations, this did not happen automatically. Some staff found suitable accommodation, while others struggled due to a lack of rental properties. For everyone, the cost of living was significantly higher than when they were living together in Delmas, and this factor greatly impacted those who didn't have adequate support.

Meanwhile, the sleepy little village experienced a sudden influx of international and local YWAM staff and students. The increase in trade delighted the local shopkeepers, cafes, restaurants, and other businesses who would benefit long term from a steady stream of new customers. During the transition time, the base leaders encouraged staff to connect with and befriend local people and businesses; relationship building was one of YWAM's foundational values.

In late December 1990 and into early January, Mark and his team quickly set up Surf Inn for the influx of forty-seven students arriving for the 1991 DTS. Several international students came early, giving them time to become familiar with Surf Inn and the school staff. Then the remaining students, including many school leavers and young adults, arrived en masse.

One moment the hotel was empty and quiet; the next, it was full of noisy, exuberant students carrying an assortment of luggage up two flights of stairs and eagerly searching for their names on room doors. There were squeals of amazement at the number of bunk beds squeezed into each room. Welcome to community living!

The school staff had been busy dealing with a myriad of last-minute details. Without the benefit of the internet, email, or cell phones, it had been time consuming connecting with students, organising the school, and setting up the dormitory-style rooms. Because there was no office when Mark and his team arrived in Muizenberg, they processed the student applications in a rented beach cottage in another village. At the same time, Mark was busy organising furniture, bulk groceries, and electricity supplies while coping with a back injury that had occurred during his army days but still caused significant, frequent pain. He hid it well.

Mark was now running his third DTS. Over time, we discovered that Jenny and Mark were kind, hospitable, and generous people. In addition, Mark had a quirky sense of humour; a few of us were left scratching our heads as we tried to work out what amused him so much.

Helping Mark run the school were Rodney Timmerman, Dave Peters, and a beautiful young Afrikaner lady, Melody Holland. This friendly, caring, and dedicated team shared briefly about themselves and their YWAM journeys. Each one viewed themselves as a servant who wanted to help us grow in our relationship with God and reach our full potential. I marvelled at the variety of people who had given up their careers or studies to serve God in this way.

Rodney was a mechanic, married to Lynda. They had two small children, Dylan and 16-month-old Talitha.

When they arrived in the Cape in 1990, they couldn't find a rental, so Mark and Jenny invited the family to stay with them. Three months later, Rodney and Lynda house-sat for friends. Just before Christmas, they found an old property that had been empty for some time. The outside was overgrown

Rodney and Lynda Timmerman and family.

and needed a good clean-up, but it was ideal for their family because it was close to the base. Once again, God had faithfully provided what they needed.

Dave was a softy-spoken Afrikaner man who had recently married a lovely lady named Kathy. She was in her element setting up the hospitality department.

Melody spoke last, sharing her mission journey and her desire to support us as we grew in our faith. Even though she was young, I was impressed by her warmth and the sense of presence she exuded. Melody had joined YWAM aged twenty in 1986, working with Mark on two schools before moving to Cape Town.

The last staff member to introduce himself was Wes, a young Canadian man. He had volunteered to staff our school until his School of Biblical Studies began in a month. It was evident that our staff were all close friends who enjoyed working together.

Three young women, Ingrid from the United States and Sandy and Belinda from South Africa, had recently completed their DTS and were assistant staff at our school. Mark explained that the base was in transition. They were still in the pioneering phase, so it was a work in progress. He also explained that South Africa was going through a tense time politically as, after twenty-seven years of incarceration, Nelson Mandela had recently been released from prison.

For YWAM staff, this was an exciting answer to many years of continual prayer for the end of apartheid. We were in a significant historical and social era as apartheid ended and the Berlin Wall came down. Both these events had been intercessory topics at the base for years. At YWAM, we were surrounded by people who looked forward to Nelson Mandela finally becoming president.

Once the staff finished introducing themselves, it was our turn. We each shared what country we were from and something about ourselves. My face had a perpetual grin. I was thrilled to be among people from so many different countries. Meeting strangers and learning about their cultures fascinated me. When I was about eight my mother had bought a set of encyclopaedias called *Lands and Peoples* for my siblings and me. We had treasured these books, as they were full of colourful, informative articles describing each country's history, lifestyle, and customs. We used them repeatedly for our school projects. My life felt surreal; suddenly I was living among people of many different cultures. This extraordinary experience was a dream come true for me.

One by one, the students stood up to introduce themselves. The common theme was that we all desired to know God more and be trained for mission work. When my roommate Judy introduced herself, I was amazed to discover she wasn't deaf at all. Mark and the staff began laughing as they watched our faces. Because we had both been told the other person was deaf, we had been facing each other to communicate, speaking slowly and enunciating our words carefully. This had provided great amusement for the staff. Over time, we discovered Mark loved practical jokes, often creating light-hearted moments for us all.

About half the students were seventeen- and eighteen-year-olds fresh out of school and still living with their families. It was exciting for them being in Muizenberg with others their age. As the area we were living in was exceptionally beautiful, I knew they would be out most weekends, exploring the vibrant city of Cape Town with all its varied attractions.

The remaining students were older locals or foreigners. Like me, they had been preparing for years to train as missionaries, giving up their homes and leaving everything familiar to fulfil the call on their life. There was a lot more at stake for us. We anticipated being trained by experienced missionaries before beginning our careers in different parts of Africa. Some of the older men were confident businesspeople. The international students had incurred the additional cost of flights, so our expectations differed from some younger students, who would return to their families or go on to university afterwards.

Mark explained the school was designed to provide a three-month lecture phase, "Getting to know God," followed by a short two-month outreach phase, "Making Him known," an opportunity to apply the principles we had learnt and put the theory into practice. He encouraged us to seek God about which outreach to join. Potential options included Russia, Brazil, Namibia, and a refugee camp near the Mozambique border.

Because the boys were attending local schools, I realised I would need to stay in Muizenberg. Even though I felt a sense of loss that I would not be able to join my friends, I was keenly aware of the importance of providing a stable home environment for the boys. Also, I was optimistic that somehow God would provide a meaningful outreach experience for me too.

Mark divided us into small groups, each with a different staff member who would be our small group leader for the duration of the school. The groups were designed to provide a sense of family, where we could share how we were doing and what we were learning and pray for each other. In addition, a journal was given to each of us to creatively illustrate the highlights and insights we gained during the lectures.

Along with the excitement of studying and living together came an awareness of inevitable challenges as we all adjusted to community life. For example, as students shared their dorms with between four to ten people, a lack of privacy and messy roommates would be a new and daunting experience for some. Thankfully, my roommate Judy was a tidy person like me. We shared a small wardrobe, a dressing table, and a narrow glass shelf in the ensuite. This truly was close living at its best!

The staff warned us about local beggars who turned up regularly when new schools began. Their targets were the unsuspecting and inexperienced foreigners who had possibly not encountered beggars before. Sure enough, during the first few weeks, several local or homeless people hung around Surf Inn with plausible sob stories, hoping to persuade us to give them money. Being experienced manipulators and knowing this was a Christian organisation, they easily quoted sections of scripture. This startled me, as it seemed so out of context with their drunken, dishevelled appearances. They'd obviously had some Christian exposure earlier in their lives and now used scripture in an attempt to manipulate the unsuspecting students.

Of course, the staff watched the same people turn up with familiar stories about needing medicine or food for a sick child and tried to warn us. But the staff's attitudes and statements sometimes sounded dismissive or insensitive to us newcomers, so we gave money. Ignoring the plight of a sick child seemed heartless. However, it didn't take long for us to realise we had been conned by experts and that the staff were experienced and more discerning than we had initially given them credit for. I was humbled to realise I had been judgemental towards the South African staff. Having ignored their warnings, the beggars easily manipulated me out of money.

Each day, we would attend lectures in the dining room: two in the morning and one after supper. Guest speakers would cover a different topic each week, including the Father's heart, hearing God's voice, guidance, studying the Word of God, evangelism, the Holy Spirit, and more. In addition, we were encouraged to record any "aha" insights and anything else God highlighted to us during the week. Completing three book reviews was mandatory. Naturally, this caused a few groans;

however, it wouldn't be a burden for me as I loved reading.

The staff encouraged us to plan fun outings together in our small groups. These special times would provide companionship and bonding. A highlight for me was discovering worship would be a regular part of our weekly timetable. I considered this to be a fantastic bonus. At this point in our orientation session, we broke for morning tea.

Holger and Dieter,
Eli's new friends.

CHAPTER 4

Curfews

After tea, the staff continued to outline different aspects of the course and how Surf Inn operated. As they shared, we became more familiar with their personalities.

During the first week of lectures, we would start with YWAM's values, which created the culture and norms on every base worldwide. So far, the staff had already mentioned worship, hospitality, servant leadership, and building strong relationships in the community.

The base extended an open invitation to locals to participate each Thursday evening in a lively time of worship, followed by a message from a guest speaker. Afterwards, everyone spent time getting to know one another. Many local people were curious about the organisation, and some were hungry to experience God's anointing instead of attending dry meetings. They appreciated being part of the vibrant weekly gatherings.

I understood this desire for more intimate times with God, as I also valued being in an atmosphere of reliance on the leading of the Holy Spirit. This season of drawing apart to spend more time focusing on God was a priceless gift to me.

Every Monday morning, we began the day with intercession and worship led by anointed musicians. At times, the presence of God washed over us with warmth and stillness that brought tears to my eyes as I contemplated all He had done for us. Some Mondays, we praised the Lord exuberantly with clapping, dancing, and loud shouts of joy.

I was thrilled to discover that prophecy was a regular part of each gathering. It felt wonderful to be among others who readily shared impressions, words, and pictures they sensed were from the Holy Spirit. I had often felt awkward about doing this in churches back home, but I began to blossom in this environment of freely celebrating spiritual gifts instead of shutting them down.

A sense of having "come home" filled me with joy. During my time in YWAM, I heard a phrase, "Go where your anointing is celebrated and not tolerated." From experience, I knew that being celebrated releases life to everyone around you, while being tolerated gradually causes you to shut down. Unfortunately, in an atmosphere of censorship, everyone misses out.

Looking around the room, I wondered how mealtimes would operate. The kitchen would have to cater for about eighty people three times a day. We were all given specific daily tasks, including vegetable preparation, serving at mealtimes, and cleaning the kitchen, dining room, and public areas.

I became part of a baking team that started at 6:30 a.m. twice a week. We baked massive batches of cookies and slab cakes for the schools and staff. Most weeks, someone celebrated a birthday, so we provided an extra cake with icing and candles. What appeared a daunting task at first soon became routine, and friendships formed quickly and easily as we worked together.

At mealtimes, we queued up to receive our food from several large metal pans. The cooks and helpers served us various dishes. The Afrikaner meals included pumpkin fritters with cinnamon and sugar sprinkled on top. Combining vegetables and sugar together was strange and didn't appeal to many foreigners initially. However, over time I came to enjoy them. Another unusual dish was "Melkkos" (milk food), which resembled lumps of dough in a thick, milky sauce. One mouthful was enough for me. I never did get used to this national delicacy, so instead we ate freshly baked bread with peanut butter and jam as a substitute meal.

A Ghanaian couple in our school struggled to eat the sweet vegetables or the pasta dishes. Understanding their dilemma, I occasionally bought them fried chicken and chips when I had extra cash. It gave me pleasure to treat them to food they enjoyed.

The portion sizes were sometimes inadequate for my growing lads, so I braced myself for their frustration when the server chose a small chicken wing for Josh or Eli. It was challenging and felt unfair when older students were tucking into juicy chunks of meat around them. I was disappointed at the lack of awareness about how much food growing boys and teenagers consume, especially when going through tremendous upheaval. Food was definitely a source of comfort at these times. With little money and no personal fridge, it became of greater importance to many people.

The mealtimes we enjoyed most were when extra food remained in the trays after everyone had been served. Soon after, the anticipated shout of "Seconds!" initiated a stampede of people hoping to score more meat and gravy. We often laughed at the intense looks on people's faces as they jostled each other to get in line. Broad smiles replaced the serious ones when the winners carried their treasure back to the tables.

Overseeing the daily running of Surf Inn were three older single ladies, who were often tense and strict. Unfortunately, this impacted the atmosphere significantly. While in New Zealand, I had anticipated training with a group of friendly, helpful, nurturing missionaries similar to John Dawson, who had encouraged me to train in South Africa. The school staff were caring and dedicated, but most leaders lived away from Surf Inn so didn't realise how much hurt and tension the manageress and her two assistants were causing. The ladies appeared to be inexperienced in dealing with both young people and the needs of families.

Feeling intimidated and vulnerable made me anxious, and I felt powerless to shield the boys when the ladies spoke to them abruptly. For some reason, I was not allowed to use the washing machines or driers but had to wash all our clothes by hand. This activity consumed quite a lot of time and was unpleasant when a cold wind blew off the shore. It was during these times we missed having our own home.

The manageress set a 10 p.m. curfew when everyone had to be in their bedrooms. I could understand this, as young ones could be noisy at night, and adequate sleep was essential to cope with our full schedule. However, there was little time to socialise, because my life was busy with classes, projects, work duties, and caring for the boys. Once they were settled, I sometimes went next door to visit my new friends. Sandra, Sue, Gerdie, and Ansie were all single South African women in their late twenties and thirties. Because the manageress checked our rooms after curfew, I was careful not to be caught. The strict, controlling environment put undue pressure on me while adjusting to the upheaval of moving to a new country and living in a large community.

Once, the manageress gave me extra work duties when she caught me out of my room, so I learned to quickly hide if I heard her approaching. One evening when I was in the kitchen, I squeezed myself between the large fridge and the wall. I thought, "This is ridiculous. I am a thirty-seven-year-old woman, squashed up against a cold concrete wall to avoid being caught out of my room."

On another occasion, when I was visiting Sandra and her roommates, we heard the manageress knock on the door. I made a mad dash for the ensuite and hid in the shower while Sandra sat on the toilet. I felt like a naughty schoolgirl, but we laughed at our crazy antics afterwards. The younger students were much bolder than me. They often snuck out the back door after room checks to spend the evening at a local Italian restaurant, where they all enjoyed coffee and bowls of delicious pasta. The curfew had not limited their social lives in the slightest. One evening Sandra and I decided we had been obedient for long enough and made our escape from Surf Inn. It felt exhilarating to break free from the restrictions as we asserted our independence and enjoyed a delicious hot coffee while Italian music played softly in the background.

Joshua, a talented self-taught musician.

CHAPTER 5

Culture Shock

In my naivete and ignorance, I was expecting to become part of a community of experienced international missionaries who had left their home countries, comforts, friends, and family and who had experienced adapting to a very different culture. Instead, I encountered a base where most staff were South African people living in their own country. This was true of my Discipleship Training School also.

South African staff members, including the leader, had been on one or more short outreaches lasting a month or two before returning to their own nation, culture, and families. They had not experienced prolonged culture shock while trying to assimilate into a different culture. Usually, they returned to their families for Christmas, Easter, or to rest after staffing a school. They ate familiar food, handled a known currency, and spoke their own language. Because their experiences were vastly different to what the boys and I encountered, they could not anticipate, identify with, or help us while we struggled to adapt.

To my surprise, I discovered there was no protocol or system in place to help single mothers like me or families with children as we went through the confusing experience of culture shock. Not understanding what was happening, I could not help my sons, so we slowly drifted apart.

The reality for the boys and I was that we were simultaneously facing several layers of culture shock. The first was living in South Africa with its diverse cultures and languages. Other challenges included not having family or close friends close by to visit, ring, or process challenges with. A big disappointment for the boys was the lack of a private place to relax as a family, which we missed a great deal and contributed to us gradually losing a sense of closeness.

Navigating the apartheid systems, beliefs, and legacy was overwhelming at times, but the joy of being in South Africa overrode these times. Often as I sat outside the front entrance, I greeted people making their way to and from the train station. I noticed black people kept their eyes on the ground as they walked past white people and looked startled when I said hello. This passive, submissive behaviour was also true of cleaners at local restaurants or maids in my friends' homes. It appeared they had learnt the art of gliding quietly around, doing what they were told and not engaging in conversation with anyone, except when their employer spoke.

I was intrigued by this oppressed group and longed to hear their stories, so I decided to begin travelling in the train's third-class carriages between Muizenberg and Cape Town. I hoped some passengers would open up and speak to me about their daily lives.

South African students warned me not to do this, believing it was dangerous, but I didn't want to live in fear of any group. I bought a cheap third-class ticket and entered the world of black labourers, maids, and gardeners. There was a significant difference between these carriages and those in first and second class. Third class carriages were very basic, with wooden forms along the sides and everyone else standing in the middle.

Most passengers averted their eyes from me. However, one lady looked up with an expression of curiosity. Her companion vacated a space, and everyone stared while I made my way to the seat beside her. I was hoping my Kiwi accent would indicate I was a foreigner who had no part in the unjust apartheid system. The men looked withdrawn and aloof, but the women seemed more open and watchful.

I began the conversation by introducing myself, "Hi, I'm Christine from New Zealand." Small talk about the weather is not my forte, especially when I wanted to learn about her life. I asked about her daily life: where she lived, her family situation, and where she worked.

I was stunned to discover she got up at 4 a.m. each morning to locate some wood, light a fire, and begin cooking her children's breakfast. After getting the children ready for their day, she began a long walk to catch a ride to the station for her train trip to one of the many white suburbs or seaside villages where she worked.

For the next eight to ten hours, she cooked, cleaned, made beds, did laundry, cared for a baby or toddler, helped get lunch ready for her employers, then looked after children when they returned from school. She fed them and picked up their belongings after them. Eventually, in the late afternoon or early evening, she walked a long way down a hill and waited for the train headed for Cape Town. Once there, she joined a queue for a bus to take her to her informal settlement and then walked the final part of the journey to her home, where she began taking care of her own family's needs.

This was a typical day's routine for most people in the carriage, whose daily lives were hard, exhausting, and relentless. Their plight saddened me.

Another challenging layer of culture shock was adjusting to community life in YWAM. Constantly being surrounded by unfamiliar people, especially at mealtimes, was difficult. Back home, the boys and I had all our meals at our dining table, where we talked about our day. It was a regular bonding time we all valued. Sadly, we rarely sat alone as a family anymore. As a result, we each felt the loss of functioning as a close-knit unit.

Nothing was familiar—not the people around us, the food we ate, the language, jokes, unspoken social norms, or clarity on the nation's history. Understandably, it was overwhelming. I felt numb at the constant need to change and adapt.

An additional struggle was learning to live without a set income. We were now "living by faith" and trusting God to provide everything we needed. Having been independent and a wage earner since the age of sixteen, it felt wrong to depend on people instead of earning a regular income. In this season, we needed Christians to respond to God's nudges and send finances so I could pay for our daily needs like rent, food, clothes, and the boys' school costs. I had hoped this aspect of becoming a missionary would be automatic and straightforward. But instead, what I discovered was that "living by faith" was confusing and quite scary at times. Due to a lack of church support, money from a few individuals came in slowly. The constant struggle caused me some sleepless nights and days of anxiety.

I was grateful to God that He enabled us to cope with the multi-faceted aspects of moving to an unfamiliar culture. However, all the challenges took their toll on the three of us. At times the boys and I felt quite disconnected from each other.

At the same time as the boys and I were going through culture shock, so too was the whole nation as they faced an uncertain future after decades of violence and white rule. The struggle to end apartheid had left millions of traumatised people with little hope of being heard or gaining justice.

Nelson Mandela was expected to become the first black president in South Africa at the next election. As forty million black people would be eligible to vote, there was no way the minority white government would retain power. It felt like the whole country was on a knife's edge as everyone's life was about to change radically. The upcoming leaders had spent decades breaking up rocks on a barren, isolated island. Suddenly, they were going to be making decisions on a national scale.

After many years of violent repression, would they retaliate with anger and bitterness? This was an era of uncertainty and insecurity for some, while others looked forward with great expectation to a new lifestyle based on equality.

The white community, who had enjoyed incredibly privileged lives with the assurance of employment, a home, a good education, and servants, had the most to lose. The disadvantaged and oppressed black majority, who frequently lived in squalor due to enormous unemployment rates—sometimes reaching 80 percent in overcrowded townships—had high hopes. With no running water, toilets, or electricity available, they expected extensive improvements to their plight. Many adults scrambled daily to earn enough money to buy food and paraffin to cook with. They stood at street corners in hot sun, rain, or cold, waiting for a white man to drive up and offer them work for the day. There was much jostling as a few lucky ones clambered into the back of a "bakkie" vehicle, relieved to be earning something for their families.

The constant stress of the blacks' desperate daily lives took its toll on their mental and physical health. Some sought relief in alcohol, while others succumbed to drugs or crime. This group hoped for a reversal of the constant struggle for the basics of life.

For the coloured group, it was a different scenario; they had been a small group between white and black people. If a black leader came to power, would they remember that the coloured group had stood alongside them during the long years of apartheid in the struggle for freedom? Or would they be overlooked? No one knew what was ahead for their group.

I was often asked about life in New Zealand as both white and coloured people began applying to emigrate to the west. They were looking for a better and more secure way of life for their families and hoping to escape their nation's expected downfall.

When we first arrived, I didn't realise the boys would automatically be categorised as "coloured" in people's eyes due to their mixed heritage. Thankfully, staff and students welcomed them and enjoyed meeting the two lads from New Zealand. At school, the boys were more aware of the outcome of the apartheid policies. Eli's school had only just opened its doors to non-whites. Unfortunately, there were few non-whites present, so he felt quite conspicuous. Meanwhile, Joshua wondered if he was just a novelty at the high school. Initially, he wasn't sure if pupils were befriending him because he was "different"", or they had a genuine desire to get to know him. With his Mediterranean looks, Josh could have passed as Greek or Italian.

The only times I was aware of the impact of separatism among the students was when an Afrikaner student commented that their parents would disapprove of them marrying an English-speaking South African. Likewise, an English student would express the same comment about their hesitation in dating an Afrikaner. It was a shame they limited themselves with close relationships when they were young, but this mindset was ingrained in them and typical in many families.

During our lecture phase, a comment made to me by a South African student shocked me so much that I was stunned for days while trying to process what she had admitted. After a lecture on different personality types, we took a test to see whether we were choleric, sanguine (extroverts), melancholic, or phlegmatic (introverts).

After the test, I spent time chatting with my Ghanaian friend, Anthony, about the results for him and his quiet wife, Hanna, who spoke very little English. Anthony surprised me by saying Hanna was a strong choleric, while he was an introvert. I had not realised this before, as he did all the communicating so appeared to be the more confident one. But he shook his head and said, "No, Hanna can be quite bossy at times." This made me laugh, as she had appeared gentle and dependent on him. Now I realised this impression was mainly due to her needing Anthony to interpret everything for her.

Later, when I shared this with my friend from Johannesburg, she looked startled and quickly walked away. Two days later, she sought me out. With tears in her eyes, she said, "Chris, when you were telling me about Anthony being an introvert and Hanna being a strong extrovert, I was shocked because until then I had never realised blacks had personalities!" Her whole worldview was rocked at this startling revelation, and she cried for two days as she came to terms with the lies that she had believed all her life. She, like many others, had been robbed of having relationships of any depth with black people, except for a few family servants.

My close friend's revelation was a massive shock to me, as I could not imagine anyone believing people existed without personalities. I grieved for both groups. Their lives were the poorer for accepting so many limiting lies. The deep injustice of these lies was mind-boggling to me, particularly as I had known, respected, and loved a black African man, whose wisdom had helped me in several challenging situations.

I, with a number of other international students, experienced forceful reactions from some white South Africans while discussing different aspects of life in their beloved nation. We soon discovered they held strong, narrow views about the black population. For example, when we commented about the many hardships the blacks endured, we were told forcefully that "they were used to this lifestyle." It was, of course, glaringly obvious to us that any human being living without running water, electricity, or toilets would desire these basic amenities, especially during the bitterly cold winter months. Personally, I was also grieved to discover how many servants lived far away from their families (including children) and only saw them for a week or two at Christmas. Our reply that no one enjoyed a low standard of living usually triggered an angry outburst of "I am tired of you bl--dy foreigners coming here and telling us how we must live." These outbursts were so unexpected that I was never sure what to do, as the person I had just upset was a new friend in a strange country, and I needed their friendship!

After a few of these fiery outbursts, we international students were baffled about why our South African friends could have a strong opinion they didn't hesitate to express, while we were not entitled to one. When discussing my dilemma with a staff member, she explained that South Africa had been shunned and criticised by the world for decades, resulting in people being touchy and defensive.

After that, I was careful not to be so forthright, knowing it would only damage friendships. Instead, I prayed for insight for those raised with apartheid lies. They needed to embrace the truth that all people have equal worth. Listening to strong views while holding myself back from sharing mine caused a sense of alienation and loneliness at times. It sure wasn't easy!

Thankfully, the boys were not encountering any unpleasant situations, but that all changed when Eli and I were at a local book shop. Each week, we collected a weekly art magazine that I bought for him as a treat. As we wandered around the shop, I heard a man's loud voice saying, "How could you?" He loudly repeated, "How could you be with a coloured person?"

Turning around to see who was saying such an insulting thing, I spotted an elderly man staring at Eli and me. My heart stopped and I was rooted to the spot with my mind racing. Eli and I had just been brazenly insulted in public. I looked at my precious, intelligent son and back to the angry little old man who felt he had the right to create a scene.

I couldn't think of a suitable reply. I was conscious of how Eli might feel, being categorised and insulted because of the colour of his skin. I wondered if I should confront the elderly guy and say, "He is my son." But I decided I wouldn't, as that might incense the bigoted accuser even more. Another option was to say, "Jesus loves us all." But I didn't, as that would possibly irritate Eli. I was so shocked that I was at a loss how to reply. I stood rooted to the spot looking quite dumbfounded until Eli took my hand saying, "Close your mouth,

Mum, you are making a spectacle of yourself!" As we walked away, my sensitive, wise young son said to me, "Did you see the old man, mum? He looked very lonely." I was amazed that he had handled the situation much better than I was able to. Being a factual choleric helped him process and dismiss it quicker than I could. But I was his mum, and someone had verbally attacked my precious son in public. That made me outraged and would take some time to get over.

I recently spoke to my Ghanaian friend, Anthony. It has been thirty years since we attended the DTS, and I wanted to know how they had been treated in 1991 before apartheid was officially abolished. I wondered if they'd had any experiences like Eli and I had encountered that day in the book shop. Thankfully they hadn't. In fact, they were welcomed and cared for by a local coloured church they'd joined when they first arrived.

Anthony commented that he observed different divisions among the whites and also among the coloured group, who referred to themselves as Cape coloured, mixed-race, or Cape Malays. This perplexed him, as most people in his country referred to themselves as Ghanaians.

Anthony and Hanna labelled people as either good or bad, not by their skin colour. He shared how, when he entered South Africa, he made a conscious decision to give himself the freedom to be who he was and not change to fit into any systems.

I admired Hanna and Anthony's worldview, which helped them retain their dignity in a nation where many had lost theirs. As I engaged with South Africans from all groups, I heard a shared desire for a harmonious society. Many individuals were reaching out across the racial divides to build meaningful relationships with each other. There was a common desire to build a better future for their nation.

Hanna Amankwah and I.

CHAPTER 6

Friends

One of the greatest joys in life is to meet someone new and then discover you either have a lot in common or you both enjoy each other's company. These effortless friendships are a gift.

My first friend in South Africa was Polly, a cockney teacher from London with a great sense of humour. Like me, she arrived days before our school began, so we got to know each other quite quickly. We were both excited about being in South Africa, where everything was different. Polly was knowledgeable about the political history and excited about Nelson Mandela's release. But the biggest surprise was her quirky humour, which I discovered when she introduced me to her travelling companion, Robert. He was a much-loved, well-worn teddy bear who tagged along wherever Polly went.

They would have hilarious animated conversations, with Polly providing both voices. My favourite "pretend" conversations were about Robert Bear's regular visits to the Queen of England. He often gave the Queen advice on national issues or commented on the misbehaviour of her children.

Polly was bright, fun, and confident. Like me, she looked forward to becoming a missionary in Africa. I enjoyed her company enormously and found myself joining in when she and Robert Bear had something to discuss. It wasn't long before we would be roaring with laughter as the witty comments became more and more outrageous.

Each day was exciting and unpredictable as Polly and I watched the students arriving. After helping them find their dorms, we would have tea together and then share our stories of how we had come to YWAM Muizenberg. For most of us, this was our first time in South Africa where everything was new and fascinating.

Sandra was my first South African friend. She was a beautiful young lady, with a good dose of self-assurance and a fantastic sense of style. From the moment we met and began chatting, we clicked. Thirty years later, we are still buddies.

I was pleased to see Sandra's room was next to mine, as it would be easy to pop in and spend time processing our experiences together. Sandra's lack of concern about people's opinions fascinated me. She didn't seem to have any desire to please people or conform to specific standards. Part of the reason came from childhood when local children had taunted Sandra, calling her names as she walked to and from school. Ignoring them became a form of protection and a way to stop the situation from escalating.

Before the apartheid era, Sandra's family had lived in the northern suburbs of Cape Town where they attended a local Catholic church. Sandra's father attended St Mary's Cathedral in the city. He enjoyed ministering to sailors, befriending them and taking them to church. Many of the homeless people he fed called him Father.

When I inquired about her parents' background, Sandra replied that her family never spoke about their ancestors, so she didn't know what nation or culture they originally came from. Her maternal grandmother died when Sandra's mother was three, so an aunt who was raising sixteen children plus three orphans took her in. As Sandra's mother grew older, any questions about her background were silenced with the statement, "You don't need to know."

Sandra's father lost his father when he was twelve. He also never spoke about his ancestors. When Sandra was fifty, she met a paternal uncle who told her that her great-grandmother was bought as a twelve-year-old slave from West Africa by a British General to serve as a housekeeper. He had two daughters by her. One of the daughters was her father's mother. The general raised his daughters as society ladies. They were both dignified women, just like Sandra. A Scottish ancestor was responsible for Sandra's father's red hair, which earned him the nickname of Scotty.

The coloured community was mainly the result of slaves from West Africa or local African women, and Malaysian servants bearing children to white sailors, soldiers, and settlers from Holland, England, Scotland, Ireland, Spain, Portugal, and Germany. There were few marriages until the government abolished slavery. White men then married the beautiful, fair-skinned, coloured women.

During the forced removals, Sandra's family was moved to a council estate called Bridgetown. Entire communities were broken up and placed with strangers from all over the Cape region. No one had any choice where they lived during this traumatic and painful time.

Because Sandra's father had very light skin, he considered himself a white person and deeply resented being moved against his will. Furthermore, it was illegal for a white and a coloured person to have a relationship or marry, so he became concerned that he would be arrested by the police. As a result, he kept to himself from then on.

In Bridgetown, the majority of incoming children had to adjust to the local schools. Fortunately, Sandra's family were able to continue at their Catholic mission school which was close by. A remarkable difference in their primary school was that the Catholic church did not adhere to separatist policies, so the nuns and teachers were from a mix of the four main groupings. Because each child was treated the same, there was no sense of inferiority or superiority among them.

During her primary school years, Sandra was aware of the other coloured children's restrictions, but her mother didn't allow her children to mix or play with them. By living a reasonably secluded life, Sandra did not experience the harsher side of apartheid. Instead, she grew into a confident and secure child while receiving an excellent primary education.

This all changed, however, when she started secondary school. By law, Sandra had to attend a local college in Bridgetown. Unfortunately, the standard was not as high as the Catholic primary school, so she often bunked classes and went to the movies or the library. By immersing herself in a wide variety of subjects, Sandra gained a broad understanding of many topics. By the time she graduated from college, she was a well-informed, independent thinker.

After school, Sandra took night classes in bookkeeping and computer skills to train for a career in administration and management. Opportunities for higher pay and better positions came her way regularly. At this time, she became a Christian and began attending a church where there was a revival happening. Later, she joined a large home fellowship that gradually became controlling and legalistic. Sandra and others were hurt by the criticism and demands of the leaders. Finally, in 1985, when Sandra attended a YWAM conference with a friend, God began to heal her.

Sandra was impressed by the teachings and values of international leaders Lauren and Darlene Cunningham. Their lesson on honouring and valuing an individual's unique calling brought significant healing to her. During the conference, Sandra felt a distinct call to missions, so she resigned from her career in 1990 and joined YWAM in 1991, when I did. Sandra was thirty-six, a year younger than me.

We both had limited support but were confident God would supply everything we needed. In the meanwhile, we appreciated the little we had. Whenever money arrived from home, I treated my boys to hamburgers and milkshakes at a local family-oriented restaurant called Mike's Kitchen. The food was inexpensive and surprisingly delicious.

Sandra and I looked forward to eating there as they had a budget "house special" that we could share. For the equivalent of a few dollars, diners could fill their plate with a

Sandra and I.

large variety of dishes at the salad bar. We soon mastered the art of creating a mountain of food that wouldn't slide off the plate as we carefully walked back to our table. Once seated, a waitress appeared with a large roasted potato, which we cut in half and shared. Because a bottomless cup of coffee was part of the deal, Sandra and I were able to enjoy one or two steaming hot cupfuls each. In this way, we paid for one meal that actually fed us both.

These outings were some of the small pleasures we looked forward to. The younger and more active students enjoyed hiking up the mountain, playing volleyball on the beach, surfing, swimming, and jamming with other musicians. Of course, we all had our favourite coffee shops, which made a roaring trade from the large group of international students.

My favourite activity was catching the train for a trip around the bay. The seascape was marvellous, with seals weaving in and out of the waves like surfers. Along the route, we passed a cottage where Cecil Rhodes, the renowned explorer, lived during his later years. His small home was preserved as a historic site and was open to curious visitors like me.

Another student who became a close friend was Sue from Johannesburg. She was beautiful, with long, blonde hair and bright, animated eyes. Sue was one of the happiest people I knew, making her a joy to be around. Her laughter and smiles were infectious. It was hard to stay upset or angry in her bubbly presence. Sue had grown up in a stable, loving home in an enormous city where most families had servants to care for the children, home, and gardens. I loved listening to her stories about the funny side of life with servants who lived in rooms at the back of the property and often became part of the family. Having never known anyone with servants, it seemed a strange but fascinating way of life to me. Sue's family was close and had a vibrant social life. She invited me to visit Johannesburg, assuring me I would be welcome to stay with her wonderful, outgoing family.

Anthony and Hanna from Ghana were an interesting young couple. Anthony was short, chubby, and friendly, while Hanna was tall, slim, regal, and quiet. Anthony spoke good English, so he communicated easily, but Hanna only knew a few words. I decided to learn some Ghanaian so I could communicate with her; in the meanwhile, we had hilarious times miming different words in an attempt to express ourselves.

Hanna's lack of English created a sense of isolation for her, which made me feel protective and motherly. When my friend and mentor Bev sent some support money, I often shared a little with Anthony and Hanna, buying toiletries or a treat. I knew they had struggled for two years to raise funds for their flights to South Africa and their visas. They didn't have the school fees when they arrived but trusted God for a miracle. I admired their dependence on Jehovah Jireh, our provider, whose grace is sufficient for the needs of every believer.

Before coming to YWAM, Anthony was an elder in his home church while running a small business. Hanna was an experienced trader, buying and selling goods. Their missions story began when a friend wrote inviting them to train at YWAM in the United States. After considering this, Anthony found it too expensive, so he applied to South Africa instead. The first step was to send their application forms to Melody, who helped them apply for study visas, thankfully granted just in time for our school.

Coming to YWAM was a gigantic leap of faith, as they didn't have any sponsors. They were a private couple who were determined to obey God as He led them to give up their only source of income and journey to South Africa. This was a courageous move for an African couple, who knew they would be entering a nation steeped in prejudice against non-whites. To their delight, they discovered God had gone ahead and prepared people like Melody, me, and others to help them.

A special person who was a source of great comfort to me during the challenging first year was Elaine Brady. She was a single mother of three girls who lived in a block of flats next door to Surf Inn. Elaine worked in a hairdressing salon in the same building. We quickly developed a close relationship, sharing our struggles and joys as single parents. Two of her daughters were the same age as Joshua and Eli and attended the same schools. Elaine and I had much in common including our desire to be involved in mission work. She attended as many community YWAM meetings as possible, which gave her a glimpse into another world. I loved her enthusiasm and eagerness to grow in her faith.

Elaine was a kind, humble, and generous person despite constantly struggling financially. Over time, I discovered that the people with very little to spare are often the most generous. Elaine definitely was. I knew God had linked us together, as her small home became a refuge for me when I wasn't coping with the more difficult side of community life. When it all got too much, I could relax, share my frustrations, and even cry if I needed to. Elaine was a wonderful gift to me. Her friendship carried me through many tough times.

Another friend was Sandiswa. She was a friendly, gentle Xhosa maid who lived in a small six foot by eight-foot room at the back of a large block of flats near Surf Inn. She had a beautiful smile and was curious about foreigners, asking questions about our home countries and why we had come to South Africa. Her Xhosa name was Sandiswa, but most maids also adopted an English name to make it easier for white employers, who often found African names hard to pronounce. Sandiswa chose the name Charity when she arrived in the Cape.

She had grown up in the Transkei Homelands, situated in the northeast of South Africa. When we met, Sandiswa was pregnant and feeling alone, as none of her family lived nearby. I could see she was anxious as she discussed her future. Thankfully, two student midwives on staff committed to supporting her during the pregnancy.

Sandiswa invited me to her home, a simple room next to two others, with an old single bed and some nails on the wall to hang a few clothes. Nothing was appealing or homey about it. Her room was located in the courtyard at the back of the flats where her employer and other tenants lived. All three occupants of the back rooms shared an outside public toilet. Because there was no bathroom, they filled a bucket with cold water and washed in their rooms.

Some of the students were shocked that I had visited Sandiswa in her room and cautioned me, "You don't befriend servants socially." However, I ignored their advice. Sandiswa and I were already friends, and she needed support.

A few weeks later, Sandiswa rang me to say her baby had been born by caesarean. Mai Banda from Malawi and I visited her, cuddling her adorable baby boy and listening to her concerns. While we were there, we met two other ladies about to have caesareans who were both very anxious, so we listened and prayed for them.

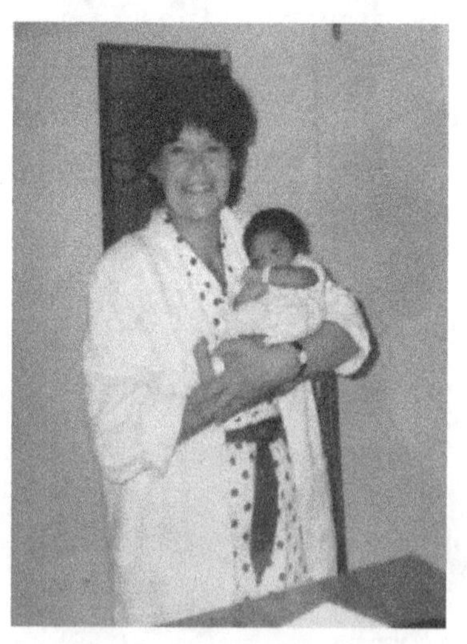

Sandiswa's baby girl.

When we returned two days later, we found Sandiswa distressed. Tenants had complained to her employer that their sleep would be disturbed when the baby cried in the night. As a result, she was instructed to return to work without the baby. The look of despair on her face broke my heart. Unfortunately, this callous attitude was not uncommon at this time. Mai and I prayed about the situation for several days while asking God to intervene.

Sandiswa's only alternative was to move to a shack out of town and sleep on the floor with the baby, so Mai and I decided to speak to her employer. He was a reasonable man, who after listening to our appeal agreed that the baby could stay with her. Mai and I were delighted and enjoyed watching the expression on Sandiswa's face when we told her. We reassured her that we would care for her like mothers. She was no longer alone. While chatting to the pregnant mums we'd met on our last visit, one of them, Margaret, told us she thought about our prayers whenever she got anxious and now felt calmer because of the assurance that God would help her. She gave me her address and asked us to visit her.

Soon afterwards, I had a ring from Sandiswa to say she was about to be discharged. It was raining heavily. Knowing that Sandiswa, the baby, and their suitcase would all get soaked through, I told her to wait while I borrowed a vehicle and came with Mai and Eli to give her a lift home. Eli stayed downstairs at the hospital and met a friendly lady on security duty at the front admission door. Her name was Vonny, and to our surprise, she took us to get food while we were waiting for Sandiswa to be released.

Sandiswa later joined YWAM and serves today in South Africa among disadvantaged groups. We are in regular contact and marvel at what has grown from a small beginning of being helped by missionaries from different nations. Their love, acceptance, and kindness made a lasting impact on her during a time of great need.

Life was surreal and full of interesting people, sights, tastes, scenery, and languages that I longed to share with my friends and family back home. But the reality was that long-distance phone calls were expensive, so I didn't hear from anyone for quite some time. However, my wonderful older sister Margy had phoned soon after we arrived to see how we were doing and to give us some family news, which I appreciated.

The lack of contact with my close friends at home made me wonder if we were drifting apart. However, that all changed one day when I heard my name being called from the phone booth downstairs. Students often sat there chatting between lectures and after meals, enjoying their free time. Naturally, they rushed to answer the landline when it rang, hoping the call would be for them. After hearing my name, I ran downstairs full of excitement and anticipation, wondering who was calling me. To my surprise and delight, it was Bev and Ian from Coniston. My dear, faithful friends knew I would love to hear from them. They were also very curious about our new lives.

It was great hearing their familiar voices with the distinctive Kiwi twang. We had a wonderful time catching up, but because I was so aware of the high cost, I talked fast, sharing as much as possible before the expensive call ended. When we said goodbye, I felt tearful and also grateful that my precious friends were so committed to us. They had represented wisdom, nurturing, and encouragement in my life for six years and now wanted to be part of my journey in Africa. Their friendship was a precious gift to the boys and me.

Bev and Ian Robertson.

CHAPTER 7

Celebrations

Being so far from our home country meant we became more patriotic and took opportunities to celebrate our uniqueness. On an Australian national holiday, an "Aussy" student wore a green T-shirt with yellow stripes made from tape. He had decorated the front with several koala and kangaroo badges. At lunchtime while we were eating, he stood up and sang "Waltzing Matilda," followed by the Australian anthem. Entering into the spirit of this enthusiastic celebration, a second student stood up and saluted him. It was great fun being entertained by these creative and spontaneous outbursts.

On another occasion, we all dressed up in Middle Eastern style for dinner, using whatever clothing or material we had. Some guys wrapped a sheet around them to

Middle Eastern dinner.

Eli with students at the beach.

resemble a toga, while the girls used fringed shawls and scarves as colourful headgear. Life was full of exciting moments like these, which we all thoroughly enjoyed.

Living near the beach provided a perfect setting for volleyball games on the white sands, surfing or swimming in warm, clear waters, and long walks in the warm evenings. People from all over the world saved for years to fly here and spend a week or two in this magnificent holiday destination. It was amazing and wonderful that we lived here and could enjoy all this beauty every day. I regularly walked along the beach, marvelling at where God had bought us to live and thanking Him because He had fulfilled His promises to me. I felt incredibly grateful to be His child.

During the first few months, as we acclimatised to our new surroundings and culture, it was inevitable that misunderstandings would cause some awkward or funny moments. A memorable mistake happened at the end of one morning's lecture when our school leader Mark announced that lunch would be a braai (barbecue) at the vlei. I assumed the vlei was a specific place, so I didn't ask any questions about its location. I originally planned to walk with my friends, but I couldn't leave with them, as my work duties kept me busy for a further half hour.

When I finally set off on my own, I was relaxed, thinking the vlei was a well-known area. But as I arrived at the local shopping area and began asking people for directions, I discovered the vlei wasn't a specific destination. Vlei referred to a large area of water. Since cell phones hadn't been invented, I couldn't make a quick call to my friends and ask for directions. So instead, I spent quite some time wandering around the lake searching for them. I felt so relieved when I finally spotted them. We all laughed about my mistake afterwards, but it had been uncomfortable feeling lost at the time.

Another uncomfortable mistake happened when a family invited us to "come for tea" at 3 p.m. In New Zealand, "tea" means an evening meal, and I assumed we would spend a pleasant hour or two getting to know each other and then sit down to a hot meal around 5 p.m. Before we left Surf Inn, I crossed our names off the list for the evening meal and happily set off with the boys.

Not long after we arrived, the wife made us a drink and presented a lovely plate of cookies. I didn't want to spoil my appetite for the main meal, so I only ate two. To my surprise, at about a quarter to five, she thanked us for coming and ushered us to the front door. Realising we wouldn't be having an evening meal with them we hurriedly said goodbye before rushing back to Surf Inn, hoping there would still be hot food for us. If there was none left, I would have to make peanut butter or jam sandwiches for us. I knew this was not an appealing option for my growing lads, as they both had healthy appetites. To our dismay, when we rushed into the dining room, the serving dishes were empty. Naturally, the boys were annoyed and became quite vocal about how I had messed up. I munched on my sandwich feeling deflated and exhausted after a long day that had ended with a furious sprint. In hindsight, I realised our invitation to "tea" meant a drink and cookies. I was careful not to make that mistake again.

The funniest mistake occurred one weekend when I overheard a student talking about the "robots" downtown. I questioned him to make sure I had heard correctly and then asked him where the robots were. He replied they were on the corner of the main road. With great excitement, I rushed off to fetch Eli, giving him the news about the robots. I knew they would be of great interest to him. Together we raced down the road until we came to the main intersection, but there were no robots anywhere. With Eli standing beside me, I asked a pedestrian if he knew where the robots were. To my embarrassment, he pointed to the traffic lights and said, "There are the robots!" Oh my goodness, I felt so foolish! I had dragged Eli downtown to see an exciting mechanical robot, when all the time "robots" were just a nickname for ordinary old traffic lights! Naturally, my son was not impressed. We both headed back to Surf Inn feeling very disappointed.

At Surf Inn we lived with many Afrikaner students and staff. This meant we heard their language regularly. It sounded harsh to me as it was quite guttural, like German. Nevertheless, the sounds fascinated me, so I decided to learn a greeting. I practised saying, "Good morning, how are you?" in Afrikaans, which sounded like "Queer-a-mora, who hun dit." Finally, when I felt confident enough to pronounce the unfamiliar words, I found an Afrikaans student to practise on. Summoning up some courage, I enthusiastically blurted out, "Queer-a-mora, who DONE IT." He looked startled but amused so I quickly replayed what I had just said in my mind. I felt foolish when I realised I'd changed "who hun dit" to the more familiar phrase of "who done it." Eek, this wasn't a cop show on television where the words "who done it" were typical. Feeling discouraged, I slunk back to my room to practise the pronunciation some more. Obviously, it wasn't as easy to speak Afrikaans as I had expected. A good dose of determination and more practice was definitely needed!

A treat out for Eli and I.

CHAPTER 8

Weekends

Some of my favourite times were the weekends, when we were free to explore the countryside. One Saturday, a carload of us went into Cape Town, where we visited the fascinating markets, fed squirrels in the central park, then travelled up the beautiful coast. Every spring, thousands of international tourists visited the coast to view the enormous blanket of colourful flowers that covered vast swathes of coastal land. Their beauty was breathtaking.

On other Saturdays, several of us participated in outreaches in Cape Town with Arnold, a tall, well-built Afrikaner evangelist. His trusty guitar was never far from his side, as he loved to worship and share about God's love with great enthusiasm. First, we met with other Christians from local churches in a nearby church and prayed for the people who would be drawn by the singing and preaching. Next, in an open area in the city centre, we sang a few songs before some students did a skit and gave short testimonies about how God's love had changed their lives. It was a good strategy; people came to listen, and the students benefited because they got used to speaking to strangers in public.

Arnold and the Outreach team.

Arnold would then launch into a passionate message about God's love and the miracle of salvation. We would all be praying silently as he spoke, knowing many people needed to surrender their lives to God's care. We could see the hurt in their faces, and sometimes tears fell as God began to move in their hearts. After inviting people who wanted prayer to come forward, we approached them and asked what their need was.

Some were ill and needed healing, while others felt lost and hopeless. I found it very satisfying to be a part of these outreaches because I loved having an opportunity to reveal God's tender love to hurting people.

As we shared our stories, we let people know that God was not a distant, demanding figure with unrealistic expectations of them. They did not need to keep striving to meet impossible standards in the hope of pleasing Him. It was a joy to share the good news that God was a loving, ever-present Father, who was always available and longing to communicate with them. Many lived with a sense of guilt or shame for years, not realising that God was always willing to forgive them when they repented. I enjoyed sharing how God had consistently guided and provided for my family.

Twice Arnold asked me to share my salvation experience in front of the large groups that gathered around us while we sang. I was surprised to discover how energised I felt when I did this. Walking through the crowd later, I found most people were open, friendly, and curious. Yet, when I met them, some had tragic stories, like one man who shared how a white policeman had shot and killed his brother in their home. The trauma and pain were etched on his face. He surprised me by saying, "If you hadn't been a foreigner, I wouldn't even talk to you." After hearing his story, I was amazed he was talking to me at all, given the circumstances.

These weekly outreaches taught me to rely on the Holy Spirit for sensitivity and courage as I approached strangers. I became aware that I had to be careful about what I said. Many people were dealing with painful issues, and I often didn't have any time to think through or prepare an appropriate response.

I was deeply moved watching people surrender their lives to Jesus, sometimes with intense emotions. Knowing they would be contacted later by follow-up teams from local churches was reassuring because the new converts would be supported as they grew in their faith.

One Saturday, a dramatic encounter happened when I introduced myself to a solemn-looking man. When I said I was a Christian, he coldly replied that he was a Satan worshipper. Gulp. I was silent because I had no idea how to respond. As I looked at him, I wondered why I hadn't noticed that he was dressed entirely in black from his head to his shoes. His outfit should have been a clue!

I quickly stilled my nerves and continued speaking with him. When he interrupted me and said he didn't care, I responded that I cared for him, and so did Jesus. However, he remained intimidating and dismissive throughout our conversation, which made it hard going for me. I realised later that even though this man stated he hadn't been listening, he remained throughout the program. I wondered if he was seeking something new to fill the void in his life that he had once hoped Satanism would fill. His situation was so tragic that I prayed and fasted for him during the following week. I knew being a Satan worshipper would not end well for this man. He definitely needed an encounter with Jesus, who was the life-giver.

My first encounter with a Muslim was with a lady called Fatima. As I tentatively approached her, I asked if she wanted prayer. I was surprised and encouraged when she asked me to pray for her daughter, whose fiery temper was causing increasing stress in their home. I shared with Fatima that Jesus had been a supportive friend to me, giving me wisdom whenever I faced a difficult situation, and in addition, he was helping me to raise my sons. Sharing a common need connected us as mothers and opened a way for Fatima to receive prayer, even though we had different beliefs.

An amusing aspect of these outreaches was watching tourists take photos and videos of us singing and performing skits. They probably believed we were all local Capetonians, but the irony was that many of us were from overseas and therefore also qualified as tourists.

After the outreaches, we visited the magnificent luxury hotels, boutique shops, and restaurants at the modern

Waterfront shopping complex. Over lunch and hot coffee, we often processed our outreach experience before heading home on the train. As I stood on the deck outside a hotel and looked up, I could see the panoramic view of Table Mountain rising to a great height in front of me. It was surreal and awe-inspiring. Previously, I had only seen this great wonder in National

Sightseeing in Cape Town.

Geographic magazines or on television, so it was an amazing experience to be standing so close to it.

Table Mountain's proximity to both the sea and the bustling city is part of what makes it so extraordinary. Its vast bulk and flat top looks like someone has sliced off the peak to create a flat tabletop. When clouds cover the top, local people comment that the mountain has its tablecloth on.

It was exciting to be in Cape Town among the vast array of cultures and surrounded by tantalising fragrances from the spice stalls in the Cape Malay marketplace. Flower sellers displayed large metal buckets of multicoloured blooms. The flower and spice markets created a gigantic mosaic of colour and fragrance that was an enormous feast for my eyes. After a painful and confusing delay of ten years, while I was waiting to come to Africa, these new experiences delighted me. They caused me to live with a heightened awareness of how my seemingly impossible dream of living in Africa had become a wonderful reality.

I savoured every moment and took nothing for granted but was incredibly grateful to God for making all this possible. I felt He had vindicated my seemingly reckless trust in Him. Having reached the exotic continent of Africa, God had proved to me that He was committed to fulfilling His promises to those who trusted in Him. I was learning that He was able to protect and provide for us, just as He had with the children of Israel. Having never travelled internationally, I had been totally out of my depth while planning this journey from my tiny island country in the South Pacific seas. I had needed God's constant guidance throughout that nerve-wracking process; thankfully, He had come through for us as a family beyond what I could ever have imagined. This experience made me eager and determined to keep moving forward on our exciting faith journey.

One never-to-be-forgotten Saturday afternoon, as we travelled home from our outreach, an Afrikaner friend, Gerdie, had a dilemma. She was holding a chocolate ice cream on a stick that someone had given her. She didn't want to eat it as it was too soft. But before long, the ice cream had turned to liquid inside the sealed packet. She looked awkward and uncomfortable, so I suggested throwing it out of the window behind her. We were in a third-class carriage which was cheaper but usually only used by non-white people. Eli called them "squash class," as they were typically overcrowded. The hard wooden bench seats ran along the carriage walls, causing passengers to face each other across the aisle.

I was sitting opposite Gerdie, watching as she worked out how to get rid of the packet of liquid in the crowded carriage. Her main dilemma was that she was squashed between two ladies, with no room to turn around. As Gerdie glanced behind her, she took aim and threw the ice cream over her shoulder, hoping it would go straight out of the open window. Unfortunately, Gerdie didn't realise that when she lifted her arm (as if doing a backstroke), the sealed packet of liquid missed the window and hit the wall above her. As the packet exploded, all the liquid began to drip onto everyone sitting in the vicinity. I watched the whole drama unfold with horror and then collapsed, laughing at the unexpected, messy outcome and the look of shock on everyone's faces.

Gerdie's face began to change as she felt something wet dripping onto her head. Cautiously putting a finger to her cheek, she scooped up the liquid and put it in her mouth. Her expression was hilarious to watch as realisation struck that the packet had split open, and the melted ice cream had landed on her head. Turning slowly to the passengers beside her, Gerdie saw that brown chocolate had covered both women's garments. By this time, her own clothes were also an absolute mess.

People opposite and around them were shocked, mouths open and eyes bulging, as they wondered why she had caused such a disaster. Some, like myself, tried to silence our laughter while poor Gerdie was frantically apologising and mopping up everyone's clothes. It was all the funnier because Gerdie was a highly organised and accomplished teacher who headed up a department at the college where she taught. Weeks later, she was still getting over the shock of her exploding ice cream.

Sightseeing with friends – Gerdie on right.

CHAPTER 9

Helping Hands

During our DTS, we went in small teams to different townships, where we worked among the community, serving them in practical ways and building relationships. For most white South African students, this was their first time relating as friends to people of colour or visiting their communities.

It was a shock for some students to find that these warm, hospitable, and trusting people were the same ones they had been taught to fear and distrust. The media had played a large part in creating fear, by portraying non-whites as violent and ignorant people.

One team spent time with families and local teachers, offering practical help. They discovered that the most pressing need was for a roof on the small local schoolhouse.

A school in need of repairs.

The lads enthusiastically began to build this, to provide protection from the rain in the coming winter months. Others chopped wood for the elderly or taught at a small school made of rough wooden poles and black plastic rubbish bags, with cardboard lining inside. The students were deeply moved by the basic conditions and many needs they saw. They helped numerous families each day with willing hearts and enjoyed playing with the excited, curious children.

The community enjoyed several dramas the students had prepared for their five-week outreaches. Presenting the dramas gave the students some much-needed practise in front of an audience. Afterwards, when a student presented the gospel message, several residents responded by surrendering their lives to Jesus or asking for prayer for healing or family issues.

The team I was part of went daily to Oceanview township (which incidentally has no ocean view at all). It was a twenty-minute drive away from Muizenberg, and vastly different in every way. Most non-white townships were tucked away from the main highways, towns, and cities. The contrast was dramatic.

Holger and I playing with kids.

We drove into a dusty, run-down settlement of about 30,000 people, which had only one rugged football ground for the thousands of children. There were no swimming pools in any schools, or parks with fun equipment. It was a barren environment overall for children and teens. However, some local people ran a children's programme, so we joined them each day.

Afterwards, the students presented dramas in a park and were encouraged to see large crowds gather quickly to watch them perform. No doubt the crowds were curious to see a vanload of white people arriving in their midst. Polly and I met a young couple who had a strong desire to motivate their community to improve the living conditions. On our visit the following weekend, we listened to their plans and spent some time encouraging them. The wife, Teresa, had a wonderful sense of humour that we enjoyed.

Many friendships were formed during the outreach, which resulted in regular visits from our new friends. They usually arrived at Surf Inn in small groups, ready to spend the day with us, sharing a meal, and enjoying our beautiful beach. We were all touched by how open the young people were as they shared about their lives, hopes, and dreams. Their visits and friendship enriched everyone's lives, especially many South Africans who had not related closely to other ethnic groups before. I imagined it would be hugely significant for them after decades of separation, suspicion, and judgment.

Following our short outreach in Oceanview, I asked my leader Mark if I could work there during my five-week outreach phase when all the other students would be away. Because townships were commonly seen as dangerous places for a white person, I thought he would say no. Instead, he delighted me by agreeing to my request.

During the last weeks of lectures, everyone was busy preparing for the outreach phase. Teams were going to Brazil, Namibia, and a Mozambican refugee camp where people had fled from a brutal civil war.

The boys and I would stay behind so their schooling wouldn't be interrupted. However, the reality was that we needed to vacate Surf Inn when the school ended, but we didn't have enough finance to rent a flat. Once again, I had a dilemma that I was dependent on God to solve. He had promised to provide for all our needs and it wasn't long before I learnt His solution to our housing problem.

While talking to Rodney (one of our school staff members), he commented that his home would be vacant for five weeks while he took a team to Namibia. Knowing our situation, he invited us to live there rent free. Relief flooded my mind at his generous offer. God had made a way for us again. Rodney and Lynda had gone the extra mile for us, as they intended to pay both the rent and the electricity costs while we lived in their home.

Words couldn't express how grateful I was to God for prompting Rodney and Lynda to sacrifice so much for us. God's love and provision humbled me and proved once again that He was absolutely trustworthy. He knew we had inadequate finances to take care of ourselves, so

He prompted others to provide where we couldn't. How could I not love Him with my whole heart and gladly follow His leading? Believing God was in control of all our circumstances gave me the courage to keep saying yes, even when the next steps looked scary or impractical.

In March a Dutch family, Rob and Marianne Vermey and their three young children, arrived at Surf Inn, with a young lady called Ruth. They had just completed a DTS outreach together and had travelled to Muizenberg after being invited earlier in the year to attend the School of Frontier Missions. They were all expecting to be welcomed and shown to their accommodation when they arrived. However, they quickly learnt that a formal process was also required before the school leaders accepted anyone. Because the leaders hadn't received the Vermeys' application forms, their names were not on the list. This was a huge shock and the start of a lonely, isolating time as they processed the unexpected news about needing to find their

Rob & Marianne Vermey and family.

own accommodation. They could only stay at Surf Inn for two nights, which was a problem as there were few rental properties in the small seaside town of Muizenberg.

Noticing the shock and distress on their faces, I quickly befriended Marianne and Rob, hoping to compensate for the cool reception they had encountered. They explained that after selling their home they joined Heidebeek YWAM in Holland, where a close community of missionaries and students worked and studied together. Initially, the Vermeys didn't even know who the base leader was there, as there was very little hierarchy or separation between base leadership and everyone else. In addition, families had their own houses on the base property, which meant the twenty children living there played together constantly while younger ones attended a creche. This freed the parents to study or work.

I was surprised to learn that mothers at the Heidebeek base were not given any work duties, and fathers only had to work three afternoons a week. Marianne described Heidebeek as a wonderful, warm, nurturing, and fun environment. Naturally, they expected the Muizenberg base to have the same values and support system for new families joining the base. Instead, they were hurt by the lack of concern or support when they arrived.

The Vermeys needed somewhere to live until June, when the School of Frontier Missions would start. Being resourceful people, they headed straight out to visit all the local rental agencies but were told each time there was nothing available. However, over the next two days they kept walking the streets and visiting agencies in nearby villages, all the time praying for help and guidance. Finally, at the thirteenth agency, they were told, "Maybe we have something for you."

With cautious optimism, they went to view a huge house in Muizenberg called Sunkist. It had been empty for two years. The house was a fantastic find; there was enough room for the Vermey family and Ruth, plus three extra rooms for other YWAM staff to rent. Together, they could afford to pay the rent of R 2,000 a month.

Sunkist multicultural community.

After speaking to several staff members, four others joined the Vermeys at Sunkist, where Marianne and Rob set about creating a YWAM atmosphere modelled on the Heidebeek base.

Each new resident arrived with a contribution of some kitchenware or furniture, and they all did daily work duties together. In addition, one of the residents was a worship leader, so worship was incorporated into their everyday life. Soon their community home was a mini Heidebeek!

Soon after moving into Sunkist a truck arrived with a load of furniture, crockery, and linen. It was all given by some township people Rob and Marianne had befriended during an outreach. When the Vermeys next visited them, they saw bare rooms and realised that these precious people, who had so little, had willingly given away the beds and tables they were using. It was humbling knowing the sacrifices their new friends had made for them.

None of the Vermey children could speak English, so being enrolled in the local schools was a significant adjustment for them. Christian had to cut off his long, blonde curls, and Judith had to tie her hair back. Even wearing uniforms was unusual for them, but they soon adapted and made friends, picking up the language more quickly than adults tend to.

I enjoyed getting to know Rob and Marianne, especially when I discovered we had many things in common, including our desire to be trained for long-term mission work in Africa. Theirs was an interesting story. After selling their home in 1990 and attending a DTS, they prepared for outreach in Indonesia. However, this fell through, so their school all came to South Africa instead. The change of plan worked out perfectly for the Vermeys, who had already decided to join the School of Frontier Missions in South Africa. This way, they only needed to buy one set of tickets.

When their team had arrived at Johannesburg airport in January, they were met by two men who loaded all their luggage plus the ten adults and children onto the open back of a pick-up truck. Driving at high speed, they began a long, dusty journey on dirt roads to a homeland called Bophuthatswana. The homeland was nicknamed "Jigsaw Land" as it consisted of several small parcels of barren land.

The South African government had moved all Tswana-speaking people to the Bophuthatswana Homeland during the apartheid era and forced them to renounce their South African citizenship. The reality was that the two million residents were dependent on South Africa for their income and resources. Half of the citizens worked in South Africa, some commuting daily from Bophuthatswana, while others lived in South Africa permanently, only visiting their families in the Homeland once or twice a year.

The Dutch team had lived and worked in these humble settings before moving to a city in South Africa. Their new accommodation was an enormous, luxurious house. To their surprise their host took them on excursions to the gold mines and tourist spots. Marianne and Rob were confused, as they hadn't given up everything in Holland to have a luxury holiday.

The team's next assignments were among coloured people in the Western Cape and in Lavender Hill near Muizenberg. By this time, they had seen a cross-section of South Africa's multicultural population and travelled almost the length of the country. Finally, the rest of the team returned to Holland, and the Vermeys came to Surf Inn to prepare for the School of Frontier Missions.

During the Vermeys' first weeks at Sunkist, I was praying for their situation when Psalm 84:4-9 caught my attention. I felt it was a significant promise to them from God.

"Blessed are those who dwell in your house; they are ever praising you. Blessed are those whose strength is in you, who have set their hearts on pilgrimage. As they pass through the valley of Baca [a dry, lonely, desolate place], they make it a place of springs; the autumn rains also cover it with pools. They go from strength to strength till each appears before God in Zion. Hear my prayer; look with favour on your anointed ones."

I decided to write out the verses, decorating them with leaves and flowers before giving them to my new friends. The verses were significant to the Vermeys who displayed them on their wall, serving as a reminder during difficult times that God's blessing was on their lives, even if it didn't always seem that way.

Having Marianne and Rob as friends brought a lot of comfort and companionship into my life. They were generous, nurturing, practical people who created a sense of close community wherever they lived. I finally felt connected with others who had the same goals and passion for Africa. They also faced many of the same challenges, making them a great couple to process with. I no longer felt I had to work everything out on my own.

CHAPTER 10

Outreaches

On a cold, windy day, I farewelled my DTS friends at the train station. We hugged and said our goodbyes as they boarded a train bound for Johannesburg in the far north to begin their outreaches in different parts of South Africa.

The teams going to Brazil and Namibia had left earlier in the week. Now, as the remaining students headed off, I felt abandoned, vulnerable, and sad standing alone on the platform. I was surprised when Wes, the Canadian guy who had assisted at the beginning of our DTS, put his arm around me as we returned to Surf Inn. He was kind and sensitive, encouraging me as we walked back. I was grateful for his words as it hit me hard that all my buddies had left. Finally, after a few tears and a welcome pep-talk, I began to pack up the boys' and my rooms, ready to move to Rodney and Lynda's home.

DTS students ready to leave by train.

I had enjoyed listening to my excited friends as they got ready for their adventurous outreaches. Melody, assisted by Sandy, took a team to Brazil to work alongside local YWAMers who ministered in favelas. Favelas were slum areas, often built on hillsides, with high crime rates and drug-related violence. Disease and infant mortality rates were high, due to poor nutrition and sanitation, and a lack of proper healthcare. With 37,000 people per square kilometre, disease spread quickly. The desire to be near the city and hopefully secure employment continually drove rural Brazilians to one of the 700 favelas. These were equivalent to South Africa's "informal settlements."

Melody's team would experience the culture of these colourful, exotic, and vibrant settlements, undoubtedly returning to South Africa with some fascinating stories to tell us. Melody had recently shared with me how she had been trusting God for finances for her flights and living expenses while on the five-week outreach. She still didn't have enough as the departure date drew closer, so she asked Mark what to do. He immediately replied, "If you don't get all your flight money, I will give you my funds." This act of generosity touched Melody's heart deeply; she knew Mark was also trusting God for finance to attend a conference in Los Angeles, yet he was prepared to sacrifice his own plans to make sure she made it to Brazil. To Melody, this act of kindness was part and parcel of who Mark Kirby was — a man full of love and grace.

A second team was heading for a refugee camp in the north of South Africa, where displaced Mozambicans lived. They had fled across the border during the 1977–1992 civil war. Due to the high number of landmines buried by warring factions, many people died or were severely maimed. This resulted in children and adults alike becoming amputees. Over one million people died during the war, and five million were displaced. Sadly, much of Mozambique's critical infrastructure was destroyed, including hospitals, rail lines, roads, and schools.

Renamo, the anti-communism factor, fought against Frelimo, the communist party backed by Russia, Cuba, and China. Several minor factions also became involved. Over time, all opposing forces were accused of human rights abuses, including using children as soldiers and indiscriminately planting landmines in many parts of the countryside. The war had traumatised many children and adults. They desperately needed help and a fresh wave of hope to lift them out of despair. I knew the DTS team would be a source of much love and kindness to the refugees.

The third team, led by Rodney and Lynda, set off by van to Rehoboth Baster in Namibia. The town, with a population of about 20,000, was founded in 1871 by the Baster people group who had emigrated from the Cape Province of South Africa. They were descendants of marriages between Boer (Dutch) immigrants and Nama (indigenous) women. The early Baster people lived in fertile areas raising cattle and sheep but were also renowned for their building skills. Today they have significant political power.

Rodney was familiar with the Rehoboth community, having led a team there the previous year. They would work alongside a local church whose focus was on building relationships with the Basters and serving the community. Their prayer was that the local people would encounter God's love. An older lady generously opened her home for the team to stay in and provided them with delicious cooked meals daily.

Belinda, a DTS assistant, led the fourth outreach to the Transkei, stopping along the way at Hogsback and then Lady Grey, where local families hosted them. Anthony and Hanna were on this outreach and were excited to meet a Ghanaian teacher in the Transkei. He invited them to join him after they completed their outreach and graduated. When I asked Anthony recently what impacted him most on the DTS, he replied it was the growth in their trust in God. They had stepped out of the boat, relying on God to provide all their needs but with no idea how He would do this. To their surprise and joy, they encountered different churches and Christians who helped them during their DTS in Muizenberg and also later when they moved to the Transkei.

The fifth outreach team consisted of only one person—me. Thankfully, I was given a vehicle to travel to Vrygrond and Oceanview townships. Even though it was lonely at times, my fascination and hunger to learn about the different people groups in the Cape motivated me to knock on doors and meet strangers, who invariably invited me inside for tea.

The outreach phase of our school had been radically changed by Mark, who decided to split the students into smaller groups instead of the usual large team heading for the same destination. Mark had a few reasons for the change. The first was that a student could "hide" in a large group and not build close relationships with other team members. In contrast, in a smaller group they had to participate. Mark found smaller groups could relate more easily, creating stronger bonds. It was also easier for the staff to notice who was struggling and support them with any challenges. Another reason for not having one large group was that the outreach phase was often spent in small towns, where a local church could have difficulty accommodating seventy staff and students.

Around the time we moved into Rodney and Lynda's home, I received several queries from friends and family about our financial needs, including our living costs. In my next newsletter, I outlined the costs we faced for the coming months in case others were interested in this information. For the five weeks we were housesitting, we needed NZ$135 per week for groceries and fuel. Other ongoing regular expenses were haircuts, toiletries, stamps, school trips, photos, and sports equipment for the boys. In addition, Josh needed a winter school uniform and shoes, plus NZ$160 was due every three months for the boys' school fees.

It was uncomfortable for me to mention money so directly, having been self-sufficient all my adult life. Writing about our living costs and letting people know how much we needed was a new experience that felt awkward and akin to begging. While chatting with others, I discovered most new missionaries struggled with this aspect. The answer was to be honest and trust God to prompt people to support us.

Soon after our DTS graduation, I applied to train at a Counselling School due to start in early June. The school involved lectures for three months, with a possibility of working in a children's home or similar afterwards during the practical phase. For many years I had been counselling troubled people, so the idea of gaining valuable skills in this area of ministry appealed to me. However, because the cost of this course was NZ$3000, I knew I would need to see a significant release of finances for the fees. Knowing God was the one who opened and closed doors, I was content to leave it in His hands and see what transpired.

I ended the newsletter with general news of life in South Africa, plus thanks to those who had become regular supporters and prayer partners with us. Receiving R 1000 in my New Zealand bank account from a tax return and the sale of some things I had left behind was a wonderful surprise, as was support money from friends.

Living by faith was an unknown experience before I arrived in South Africa. It seemed precarious and unpredictable most of the time, with no set formula for having money in the bank when it was needed. I relied on God's promises, such as, "No good thing does He withhold from those who walk uprightly" (Psalm 84:11) and "But seek first the Kingdom of God and His righteousness, and all these things will be added to you" (Matthew 6:33). I trusted that "all these things" referred to rent, food, and clothes!

Having no means to provide financially for us any longer was a steep and sudden learning curve. In later years I learnt that some mission organisations insist missionaries raise a certain amount of financial support monthly before being accepted for training. Having experienced the opposite, with its accompanying anxiety and stress, I think raising supporters first is helpful. However, in situations like mine, where the home church was not supportive, it is sometimes necessary to just launch out and trust God to provide. As I had spent the first ten years of my Christian walk responding to God's nudges, I continued to do this. He had always been faithful to us, so I trusted Him to keep guiding me in this new area of no set income. His creative ways of doing this were wonderful and deepened our trust in Him.

When all the financial props are removed, you quickly learn where your security lies. I realised that as much as we would like an abundance of most things, God has a plan to mature us in the area of trust. We can't be wrapped in cotton wool if we desire to grow in faith. The hard times are necessary, as they reveal what's in our hearts and quickly separate the dreamers from the committed ones. I was grateful and appreciated every person who supported us while I trained with YWAM. It had become a true partnership of the "senders" at home helping me during each essential phase. A song that expressed what I was learning stated "Every day, I look to you to be the strength of my life; you're the one I hold on to, to be the strength of my life."

Before moving to Rodney's home, I knew we would not have enough money for food or unexpected expenses and had no idea where the money would come from. During a conversation with Marianne and Rob about my financial situation, Marianne surprised me by saying they both had decided to give us their tithe money. I felt quite teary at their commitment to us at such a crucial time of need. My anxious heart relaxed! God had prompted Rob and Marianne, and they had obeyed. This act of obedience on their part blessed us as a family. I felt gratitude for their love and concern towards us, and deep love for my Heavenly Father who had nudged them to invest in us.

CHAPTER 11

Oceanview

After moving to the Timmermans' home, I spent a few days settling in and praying about the outreach. It was wonderful having so much room to ourselves and being able to cook familiar food again. In addition, the boys enjoyed the closeness of just the three of us living together instead of having many others around.

We were shocked when we first saw the house. It was a large, older-style white concrete building with all the windows covered in thick, rusty burglar bars. In addition, the front and back doors had high metal security gates that were kept locked. All the bars gave the concrete house the look of a prison. In addition, I had to unlock the security gate, then unlock a wooden door and relock it all when I left or came home. We had never seen any house windows fortified with thick metal bars back home. Unfortunately, it was the norm in South Africa due to extremely high rates of rape and murder. Instead of making us feel safe, it was a horrible reminder of the high daily crime rates.

Burglar bars.

My friend Marianne commented that people constantly lived with high levels of fear and anxiety. Because so few had lived outside their own country or experienced culture shock, they were limited in their understanding of what it was like for anyone moving into their nation.

Whenever a vehicle was available, I borrowed one to travel to either Vrygrond or Oceanview. Both were low socioeconomic settlements of coloured folk. The first township I visited was Oceanview, where I decided to simply start knocking on doors, introduce myself, and see what unfolded.

The first residents I met were a delightful elderly couple called Gilbert and Maggie. It was very unusual to see a black person living in this coloured township, but Gilbert was permitted to live there because his wife was coloured. Having already been married for several years when apartheid was enforced, they had been allowed to stay together. Gilbert and Maggie were a friendly couple, who invited me inside for a cup of tea and a chat. I enjoyed their company so much that I visited them regularly during my outreach. Their welcome each time made me feel like they had adopted me! One Sunday, I met several of their family when I arrived for lunch. I was treated like a guest of honour in their small home, being served tea in a delicate china cup and food on a beautifully laid-out tray. Every effort was made to make me feel welcome and special.

Gilbert fascinated me. He was a confident man who was at ease with me from our first meeting. The explanation was simple. During the Second World War, when he served in Egypt, Gilbert had met many Kiwi soldiers who became his friends. So meeting me, another Kiwi, many years later delighted Gilbert, who chatted away to me like a close friend. He was an intelligent, knowledgeable man who communicated easily and well. No doubt his career at the naval base in Simon's Town for forty-seven years had provided him with many opportunities to speak with sailors from many nations.

When I asked how they had ended up at Oceanview, Gilbert told me their story. Thirty years beforehand, during the apartheid era, every person of colour was rounded up and forcibly removed to one of several settlements on barren ground. Gilbert and Maggie had owned their own home near a beach and had enjoyed a healthy lifestyle, fishing and swimming with their children.

One day, while Maggie was in hospital and Gilbert was home with their four young children, soldiers arrived in a truck to forcibly remove the family from their home. The soldiers refused Gilbert's request for an extension until Maggie had recovered and returned. Instead, they told him their belongings would be put outside in the rain if he didn't pack immediately and vacate his home. In deep shock, Gilbert had to begin emptying his house of all its contents.

A friend came by with a truck and helped pack everything up. The china, bedding, kitchenware, furniture, and clothes were piled high in a chaotic mess. Army trucks took thousands of traumatised people to a sandy site, where hastily constructed three-storey flats and other dwelling places stood waiting for the new tenants. Access to the top flats was by a narrow outside wooden staircase, so the larger pieces of furniture were broken up if they couldn't be appropriately dismantled. Gilbert told me that some older people died from the shock of being uprooted from their family homes and losing familiar neighbours and friends.

In those early days, there were only a few small shops but no transport service, which meant Gilbert and others walked daily for over two hours each way to the naval base at Simon's Town. I tried to imagine what it would have been like for everyone, especially on cold, dark, wet winter mornings.

When I asked Gilbert if they were bitter or angry, he told me he had initially been angry, but that feeling had passed over time. His outlook on the terrible injustices he faced was to make the best of the situation. As the weeks progressed, I discovered forgiveness was a common thread among the many people I visited, especially those who loved God. They were determined to make the best of their new life.

The residents of Oceanview taught me some valuable life lessons. Overall, I was deeply affected by both the plight and the sense of resilience I experienced among the residents of Oceanview. It was an enlightening time that made me incredibly grateful for hot showers, roomy buildings, and nearby transport. I never took these simple things for granted again.

The settlements that shocked me most were the enormous, sprawling squatter camps populated by

Xhosa and Zulu people. As I drove through one called Crossroads, I was stunned by the many acres of rudimentary shacks made of rough poles, scrap wood, and plastic, with old metal sheets creating a roof held down by huge rocks. Each hut was cobbled together by whatever cast-off materials could be found. The Vermeys, who had driven past Crossroads settlement some weeks before, told me they had thought the shacks housed horses and cattle. They were shocked to learn that people lived there. The residents I met were generally unemployed rural people who had moved nearer to the city hoping to create a better life for their families. Instead, they had to compete for a tiny piece of land on rough ground, on which they hastily erected a shack that lacked running water, electricity, or a toilet.

Crossroads.

I felt saddened as I watched men cutting branches off trees for the women to carry in bundles on their heads. Old cardboard and pieces of wood were used to reinforce their draughty homes against the cold, fierce Cape winds that blew in winter. There was a local saying that the Cape was like a baby — either wet or windy.

The lives of people living in these squatter camps were extremely difficult, far removed from the average white person's experience. Yet they served their madams with a calm demeanour and were kind to the children and loyal to those employing them. This was a mystery to me at first, but after witnessing several acts of kindness by employers, I understood. Employers often paid for their servant's medical bills, the children's school fees and uniforms, and a variety of other needs. In a land where unemployment rates were extremely high among disadvantaged groups, maids and gardeners valued their secure jobs.

There was often a long-standing relationship and two-way commitment between servants and their employers. Unfortunately, there was also widespread abuse of employees, because they were vulnerable and so desperate that they wouldn't risk their jobs by complaining.

Train conversations gave me a more rounded view of the lives of those living in squatter camps. They were the invisible millions who were also the backbone of the nation.

CHAPTER 12

Vrygrond

The second township I worked at was Vrygrond (free ground), where I assisted a lady running a sewing class. The amenities were basic, but the ladies were keen to learn a new skill that I was fortunate enough to have been taught at school. Having sewn clothes for myself and the boys for many years, I knew the pleasure that came from creating something lovely. It was a joy to encourage and work with each of the ladies, knowing they too would one day be proud of their achievements for their families.

Next to the sewing building was a preschool where many children spent much of the day playing outside in the sand dunes. As I began spending more time with the young children, I realised they didn't have any toys to play with. The next day, I returned with simple scoops and containers for the children to create sandcastles. I'd made them by cutting large plastic fizzy drink bottles in a specific way to create a scoop with the handle from the top segment, while the bottom half of

Preschool in the sand dunes.

the bottle became a little bucket. Because the children had a great time playing with them, I was motivated to create or buy more equipment like skipping ropes and plastic balls.

Attached to Eli's primary school was a preschool. I popped in one day to meet the teacher and introduce myself. After explaining the plight of the Vrygrond children, she invited me to bring them to her preschool for a day to play with the white children and enjoy the vast array of bright, colourful toys and bikes. I was delighted at her offer and quickly made arrangements with the Vrygrond teacher, who accompanied the children on their outing the following week.

It was fascinating to watch the coloured children, who stood quietly to one side, while observing the white children, who were animated, confident, and outspoken when speaking to their teacher. They, too, were fascinated by the new arrivals.

Gradually the visiting children began to try out the bikes and scooters, smiling and calling out to one another as they whizzed around the concrete track. Our host teacher had organised various activities, which made for a fun-filled day.

I longed to provide resources for the Vrygrond children, but finances only allowed me to buy crayons and paper. Over the years, I saw many preschools like this, where the children spent long days with untrained carers, who were doing their best but could not provide resources to stimulate or teach the little ones. The apartheid policies had created an enormous disparity in education between the different groups in South Africa.

I met a family during my time in Vrygrond who told me a shocking story. Velicia, the mother, gave birth to a baby girl in a hospital. When the baby was two days old, a Muslim lady who Velicia used to work for took them to her home. Velicia was happy, thinking she was about to be given some new clothes for the baby, so she willingly accompanied her ex-employer. However, when they arrived, the Muslim lady took the baby from Velicia and handed the newborn to her son and daughter-in-law, who promptly drove off in their car.

After the baby was kidnapped, Velicia had to walk a long distance home, feeling distressed and in shock. Finally, she and her husband went to the police station to report the incident, but the police refused to help them. They sought help from a social worker who heard their story but didn't take action either. Velicia was crying when she told me she had not seen her little girl since she was two days old.

Velicia and her husband Joseph were a gentle couple who couldn't read or write, which added to their sense of inadequacy and powerlessness. They were overwhelmed by their situation and didn't know what to do next. I promptly rang the social worker to verify their story as it sounded unbelievable, and she confirmed the baby had indeed been kidnapped. She told me the Muslim lady also had Velicia's bankbook and was withholding her monthly disability allowance. In addition, the Muslim lady constantly threatened Velicia and Joseph, using intimidation to silence them.

I was outraged at the social worker's casual manner and lack of action. I asked her, "What are you going to do about this appalling injustice?" She calmly replied, "Yes, it is a problem," but didn't indicate whether she intended to help them. I was outraged. I let her know I would not ignore their plight and would be contacting her soon to ask what action she had taken.

At the end of the call, I felt disgusted and frustrated with the whole situation. All I could do was reassure Velicia that I would keep pursuing justice for her. After driving

Velicia home, I was saddened to see how they lived. Their home was a single rented room in a huge house, with many families like them each living in one room. The only furniture Velicia had was two single beds — one for the grandmother and six-year-old Patrick to share, the other for Joseph and Velicia. The floor was bare, and there were no curtains at the windows.

Leena, the grandmother, was a gentle Christian lady, who often smiled and said she was "satisfied," even though she was blind due to diabetes. Knowing how little the elderly received for a pension, I guessed Leena felt fortunate to be with her family, who loved and cared for her despite the added cost of feeding a fourth person. Unfortunately, the family usually ran out of food in the third week of each month, increasing their daily stress. I decided to try and push for a better place for them to live once we sorted out their dilemma concerning the baby.

With over 32,000 people desperately needing adequate housing in the Cape area, finding affordable rental accommodation was an enormous challenge. Over the next few weeks, I made two trips to the Cape Flats Development Association (CAFDA), who handled social and community issues. Just before 7 a.m., I drove to Wynberg and sat on a hard, narrow wooden bench in a cold room. I took a grubby, crumpled card with a number on it as I entered. Those who arrived very early got the first numbers and were seen before lunchtime.

Not us—we sat for hours with people around us chatting in Xhosa and Afrikaans. I couldn't help but smile at the hearty laughter around me. When we finally got into the interview room, I sat quietly while Velicia and a new social worker spoke in Afrikaans. Whenever there was a gap in the conversation, I would ask Velicia what was happening. At the end of the interview, I encouraged the social worker to take the necessary action to retrieve the baby and return her to Velicia and Joseph. I hoped my presence would make a difference, as Velicia had previously met with indifference.

During the interview, Velicia informed the social worker that she had been thrown out of a second-storey window when she was little, suffering minor brain damage. I was shocked and felt it was a miracle she had survived. Thankfully, her disability was not severe, but it impeded her ability to concentrate. Each month the government supplied a small disability grant of about NZ$30, which unfortunately was used by the Muslim lady who held the bankbook. I appealed to the social worker to cancel it and issue another one for Velicia, but her detached expression didn't raise my hopes for any much-needed action.

To our surprise, a different social worker retrieved the bankbook a few weeks later and returned it to Velicia. This compassionate lady assured us she was determined to bring the baby home. I was relieved that, at last, someone in authority was committed to helping Velicia and Joseph.

As they talked with the social worker, Velicia expressed concern about her ability to provide for the baby and commented it might be best for a loving couple to adopt her. Sadly, I could see she was aware that limited finances would make it difficult to feed and clothe an additional child when they were already struggling every week just for food. My heart went out to her as she grappled with the realities of their difficult situation. I prayed for God's guidance as they made decisions for the future.

During the last week of outreach in Vrygrond, my Dutch friend Marianne and I borrowed a car so we could visit a family whose children needed school shoes. However, once we arrived and began looking for their home, we discovered it wasn't easy to locate. The family lived among a collection of ramshackle old flats and hastily erected shacks.

Before setting out, locals warned us it was dangerous for white people, especially women, to go there. However, we weren't concerned because we hadn't grown up fearing people of other cultures. When we arrived, some residents told us they knew where the family lived, so we followed them through the crowded, tightly packed shacks until we reached the children's home. Seeing the joy on their faces as they tried their new shoes on was terrific and made all our efforts worthwhile.

Years later as she looked back on this visit, Marianne realised we had been unwise, as drug dealers and rival gangs lived there. Over time, we heard of many people being robbed and attacked in the townships. Once again, God had protected us, for which we were very grateful.

During the following weeks, I was on outreach at Oceanview. Sadly, I never saw Velicia again. I wondered if they had moved away after deciding to leave the baby where she was loved and had better prospects for her future.

Some situations I encountered were so harrowing and overwhelming that I felt numb for weeks afterwards. Velicia's story was definitely one of those. As I processed their situation later, I wondered if my role had been to just support and love her while she sought justice and gained strength to make a heart-wrenching decision that would remain with her for life.

I recently read a caption: "Some friends are for a season, some for a reason, and some for a lifetime." I had no doubt I was placed in Velicia's life for a specific reason and a short season. All I could do was let go and hand their situation over to God. It was not easy, but I needed to trust Him for the right outcome.

Knowing I was approaching the end of my DTS experience, I wondered what the next step would be. I was conscious of the boys' need to remain at the local schools. They were developing good friendships, so I didn't want to uproot them again.

While pondering our future, I heard that YWAM was running a Counselling School from mid-June to September, with placements from September to December. After applying, I was delighted when the school leader, Hugh, contacted me with the news I had been accepted as a student.

At the end of my five-week outreach to Oceanview and Vrygrond, we began packing up the Timmerman's house since they were due back from Namibia. It was time for us to move back into Surf Inn. The other DTS staff and students were also due to return from their various outreaches. The boys and I looked forward to seeing them again and hearing about their adventures. The five weeks of house-sitting had been a special time where we had regained a sense of being a family unit.

In Vrygrond and Oceanview, I had experienced God connecting me with people and organisations that I hoped to work with in the future. I had learnt to trust God as I stepped out into the unknown. I was discovering that all I needed to do was simply drive to the townships, then enjoy watching God unfold the next part of his plan! By doing this, I found that the anticipation of a new adventure energised me. I actually thrived on meeting strangers and connecting with them as they shared their stories. This had also been true in New Zealand, but I only realised it during my time at these townships. I wondered why it had taken me so long to discover this obvious fact about myself!

Eli enjoying the beach—creative sand sculptures.

CHAPTER **13**

Preparation

After applying for the Counselling School and being accepted, I had to trust God for both my school fees and the living expenses for the three of us.

Even though I was eager to become more skilled as a counsellor, the reality was that I was not keen to move back into Surf Inn, as it had been a difficult experience for us during my DTS. In addition, dealing with the many rules and the strict, unpredictable management staff created unwanted stress.

Apparently, I'd had an unusual experience. A staff member informed me that single mothers usually didn't have to share a room with anyone else and weren't given any work duties. This allowed them to concentrate on their families, as they all underwent the same significant adjustments the boys and I had. On hearing this, I realised I had definitely been through a challenging introduction to YWAM life.

I talked to Hugh, my Counselling School leader, about our earlier experience in Surf Inn. He thoughtfully ensured I was given a sunny room to myself, with a sofa for the boys when they visited me. Hugh also arranged an exemption from all work duties.

Another bonus was that I was given access to the washing machine and dryer at a low cost. The days were colder with winter approaching, so I was grateful that I wouldn't be washing our clothes by hand and hanging them outside when nippy winds were blowing. These significant changes made a massive difference and meant I was more relaxed about moving back into Surf Inn.

Soon after moving in, Eli and I developed painful boils. Eli then became sick for a few days with a fever and swollen larynx. Thankfully we both recovered quickly and regained our strength. Meanwhile, Josh was given a black eye in a freak accident with another pupil at school. Actually, it was more purple and pink than black!

As I prepared for both the return of the DTS students and our graduation, I felt privileged to have been accepted into the small Counselling School. My hope was that it would equip me in counselling and enable me to work in township clinics in the future.

Life became increasingly busy and noisy as the outreach teams arrived back. It was exciting greeting friends and sharing our experiences of the past five weeks. Each team went through a time of processing their outreach experience, starting with their expectations before they left Muizenberg.

For some, their trip was fulfilling; for others, it had been a disappointing and frustrating experience. Anthony and Hanna had thoroughly enjoyed their time in the Transkei, where they'd met a Ghanaian pastor who asked them to join him after their graduation. Polly and Sue returned full of smiles, with interesting stories of the people they met and befriended on their outreach to Namibia.

Unfortunately for Sandra, her outreach to the Mozambican refugees had not been anything like she had imagined. Instead of being involved with the refugees, the team remained on the farm that was hosting them doing practical work. As a result, trips to the refugee camp were infrequent, making for a frustrating and disappointing experience. Sandra had sacrificed so much to train in missions, with her heart set on Russia. Unfortunately, she was gradually losing hope that this was going to happen.

After our graduation, Mark asked how the DTS had been for me. I explained the difficulties we had encountered in staying connected as a family while sharing a room with another student. He replied that it was an experiment that wouldn't be repeated. In 2021 when Mark and I reminisced about the DTS, he shared how the staff had prayed for the best way to accommodate us as a family. Logistically, it was a challenge for them due to the high number of students and staff and the limited rooms available.

The days following our graduation were a time of teary goodbyes as students departed for their hometowns or other nations. Several of the younger ones had formed relationships that made them reluctant to part, while others went on a holiday before joining the staff for the upcoming schools. It was an intense and emotional few days. Then suddenly, there was resounding silence in Surf Inn, with only a skeleton staff plus the boys and me left there.

While it would have been lovely to have had a break between my outreach and the upcoming Counselling School, it was not possible due to the now-familiar problem of limited funds. I longed to explore Cape Town and enjoy a holiday with the boys, but we only had a week before my new school started, and all the rooms needed to be set up for the four small schools about to begin. I was given the option of free accommodation and food for us for the week in return for helping to clean, set up, and organise Surf Inn for the incoming schools. I had hoped someone would invite us for a week's holiday at their home, but this didn't happen. I decided that the offer to work in exchange for accommodation and meals was God's provision for us.

An exciting yacht ride with friends.

It was now early June, and I was weary after an intense five and a half months. I prayed for God to strengthen me during the mammoth task of moving bunks and other furniture around. Thankfully I was fit and optimistic, and I applied myself each day to working hard. To my surprise, the manageress became more relaxed, which meant we got on very well. We even had some fun times together, making the tasks more enjoyable. I saw a softer side of her now that the relentless daily grind of running a twenty-six-room building and feeding a horde of hungry young people had ended.

Towards the end of the week, when the manageress became unwell and spent a day in bed, I had an opportunity to pamper her with some special food and the gift of a coffee mug. I was surprised when she opened up and shared how unhappy she had been in her position as manageress. It was a lonely, demanding role. To my surprise, she apologised and became more flexible and helpful to us as a family. I repented to God for judging her so harshly and not reaching out to her in friendship. Other staff helped us to complete the rooms on time.

I felt relieved that all the rooms were ready when the students started arriving. Some, like me, were returning to do a second-level school. Josh and Eli were looking forward to having some young folk around again, while I was eager to begin my course.

After a few weeks of having little cash to spare, I received support money from my family, which was terrific. When money arrived from New Zealand, I usually took the boys to our favourite family restaurant, Mike's Kitchen, for a treat of tasty hamburgers, chips, and milkshakes. The boys tucked in enthusiastically while I looked on, appreciating the opportunity to spoil them. Receiving money sporadically meant I couldn't plan events, so we made the most of these surprises. I felt it was important to create regular highlights for Josh and Eli, as they had sacrificed so much in coming to Africa. Assimilating into their schools and the YWAM culture was sometimes a struggle for them.

It felt like Christmas when my brother Donald in England sent us twenty-five pounds a few days later. How fabulous that so many people had decided to send money simultaneously! The timing was perfect, as my next financial priority was paying the first instalment of my Counselling School fees.

Imagine my joy when Robert Hudson, the registrar, informed me I had been given a 50 percent scholarship. Hallelujah! This fee reduction was a great gift, as the school fees included accommodation and food for the three of us and meant the total cost had been reduced to just under R 3000, equivalent to NZ$300. Furthermore, it meant I could pay the total off quicker. The next day I happily paid the R 600 deposit and thanked the registrar for the unexpected news and the generosity of whoever made that decision.

Walking back to Surf Inn, I felt I had been through a test to learn where my source of income and security was—God. I thought of the verse, "Seek ye first the Kingdom of God and His righteousness and all these things [our daily needs] will be added to you" (Matthew 6:33, emphasis mine). God did care. He saw what we needed and provided it in His own unique way and time. God was seldom early but never too late!

The boys were on their own journey, adapting to life in a mission community setting and experiencing the unpredictability of living by faith. It was to be expected that this got too much for them at times. I knew they longed for the stability of a working mum who earned a regular wage, but that season had ended.

Before leaving New Zealand, I had underestimated the wrench of moving Josh and Eli across the world. I had assumed they would be as excited by our adventure as I was. But that was naive and overlooked the fact that while I had a constant compelling drive to train in mission work in Africa, the boys didn't. It was my dream and my calling, not theirs. They missed their nana, their friends and cousins, and living in the privacy and freedom of their own home.

At times I felt overwhelmed by what I had forced the boys to do, but I had to keep trusting God that He would enable them to endure and adapt to our new life. I reasoned that if God called me to Africa, then he also had a purpose for the upheaval the boys were experiencing. I needed to remain steady and confident in God's wisdom, compassion, and guidance. Thankfully the boys developed close friendships among the students and at school, plus Joshua was ecstatic about living by the sea.

I wasn't sure how the boys were doing at school, so I was relieved when they showed me their mid-year exam results. Eli scored 90 percent, achieving the highest maths mark in his class. He had coped very well with the different style of education. His teacher confirmed this, informing me that Eli had completed all the work she gave him, including his Afrikaans subjects. His ability surprised her but made her realise the New Zealand education system was quite different from the South African rote-learning style. Eli's teacher told me that our school system had encouraged Eli to think independently and solve problems from an early age. When she set this type of exercise for the class, he invariably finished first.

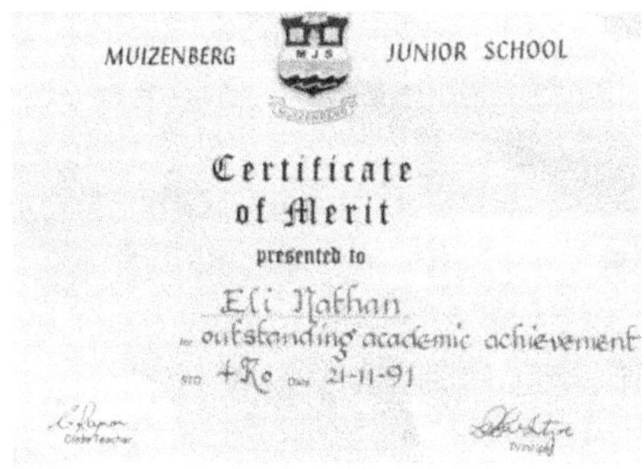

*Eli in school uniform
and excelling at school.*

Josh also received a positive report saying he had improved a great deal academically. At a parent-teacher feedback time, I was delighted to hear him described as a gentleman. I agreed. Josh was a bright lad and a gifted musician who had taught himself to play both guitar and drums.

One afternoon in Surf Inn, I heard some lovely piano music coming from the lounge. When I opened the door to see who the musician was, to my great surprise I saw Joshua confidently playing the piano with both hands. I was dumbfounded, as I had not seen him even try out basic chords before. When I asked where he had learnt to play so well, he told me he had spent hours exploring chords on my mother's piano as a child and had recently begun composing tunes. I realised he had inherited this ability from my mother, who was a gifted musician as a child. She later trained as a concert pianist.

As their mum, it was heart-warming for me to watch the boys relax and grow in their faith as they saw God answering our prayers and providing for us again and again. Initially, Eli was worried and upset when we moved to the Timmer-man's house, telling me we were poor because we didn't have a home and I didn't have a job. Watching us run out of food or

Josh the gentleman.

money at different times was stressful for him. But once he was settled back into Surf Inn, he relaxed and enjoyed playing with the other children living there. I discovered that as much as I wanted to protect the boys from difficult times, I couldn't. They also needed to learn their own valuable lessons. Over time, Eli became part of a group of boys who invited him to their homes on weekends. His special friend was Ryan, who is still his close buddy thirty years later!

An essential part of missionary life that I struggled with was regularly composing newsletters. Friends and family naturally wanted to know how we were doing and what life was like, while I needed them to pray and support us financially. As there was no internet in 1991, the only option was to carefully edit our experiences and present an interesting overview of the previous few months. In addition, I knew it was necessary to send informative newsletters to build up a following of prayer and financial supporters, which were both crucial. But oh, the effort involved! I would begin, get stumped, procrastinate for days or weeks, then start again, before finally coming up with a sanitised version of the enormous daily challenges, the anxiety when funds were scarce, or the loneliness that swamped me at times.

I didn't want my family to worry about us, so I skipped over most of the difficult experiences and instead presented a happier version of our lives, focusing on the highlights. I often dreaded writing. It took a lot of precious time and effort to compile the newsletter, plus it was emotional revisiting some of the difficult situations. Once I began, I often wrote far too much, then had to redo it to reduce the size. Fortunately, after sending the handwritten newsletter to Bev in Coniston, she photocopied it many times and posted it to a long list of people for me.

It is interesting how emotional I feel now as I vividly remember those times so long ago. It is probably because the pace of life was so fast that I rarely had time to stop and process anything during my first years in missions. At times it all felt like a big blur. I am incredibly grateful that I have my journals to supply all these stories. My buddy Bev kept every newsletter plus every personal letter or postcard I sent to her and gave them back to me when I came home in 2013. That act was a priceless gift and has given me abundant material to weave into my books.

Whenever Bev called, I felt comforted and valued at hearing her voice. She was the one who knew me best and had lovingly supported me through many difficult times in New Zealand while championing my vision; now she still consistently reached out with love and encouragement. Her ability to listen patiently and offer wise words of comfort was a powerful gift throughout my mission career.

The week before the new schools began, a quietly spoken Afrikaner man arrived with his team. He was the leader of the School of Evangelism. Within days, the whole atmosphere of Surf Inn had changed. Gone were the petty, restrictive rules, and in their place was flexibility, generosity, and a sense of value towards each of us as we encountered Francois's kindness and humour. Previously, food was often restricted to three meals a day, but now a table with hot bread, butter, and different spreads was available twenty-four hours a day. Because it was hard to resist eating the hot bread smothered in peanut butter and jam, most of us gained at least five kilograms during our school.

Francois had spent years organising and leading large outreach teams of young people around southern Africa. He was relational and fatherly in his approach to situations and easily created a warm, fun family environment. The most significant change I saw was the softening of the manageress. She was happier and walked around with a big smile on her face. Instead of feeling overwhelmed and alone, she was now among her own people, in a close relationship with the school staff. I imagined she felt more supported. It was fascinating to watch her transformation. I soon discovered that Francois ran a large boarding house in Pretoria with many young people, mainly young men, who often stayed with him for years. He was a wise older man who many students and some staff called Pa.

Charles Reed.

Among the residents of Surf Inn was one of the happiest young guys I had met. Charlie was mischievous, demonstrative, fun, and full of joy. He came from Durban, another famous surfing destination. Charlie, to my delight, immediately gravitated towards Josh and Eli. Having been a youth leader, he was experienced in building relationships with young people. Whenever he bounced into a room, you couldn't help but smile. He exuded fun and positivity wherever he went. Charlie and the boys spent hours in their room happily chatting and laughing while they created all sorts of vehicles and buildings using Lego blocks. It was great watching the boys relaxing with him and others.

I was thrilled that my good friends Sandra and the Vermeys also moved into Surf Inn in preparation for their three-month School of Frontier Missions. The Vermeys planned to form a team and travel to Malawi, where they hoped to work long term among the Yao people. Meanwhile, Sandra was once again concentrating on training for a future in Russia.

After completing the Counselling School in September, I hoped we would have enough regular support to move into a small flat. I felt this was important for us, especially Josh, because he would be studying for his final exams the next year. In South Africa, most students stayed at school until they were about eighteen and had passed a rigorous matric exam. Matric was the final exam at secondary school. If a student failed, they often kept trying until they passed. It was difficult to get a desirable job or further their education without a matric pass.

In contrast, back home in New Zealand students sat a School Certificate exam, around age fifteen or sixteen. Those who wanted to study further remained at school for one more year to prepare for the University Entrance exam. However, many students left school after the School Certificate exam (whether they passed or failed) to begin apprenticeships in various trades. Others entered secretarial schools or started careers in nursing or dental work.

In New Zealand, there was no shame in leaving school after sitting School Certificate. In fact, those who stayed at school were often envious of those who left early and immediately began earning a wage, albeit a small one. These teens had become independent, while we still donned our unflattering uniforms every day and trudged off to school lugging heavy bags.

In South Africa, there was enormous pressure for everyone to pass the matric exams. Students often felt shame if they failed. I met adults in their mid-twenties who were still studying part-time to pass matric! It was the benchmark, the coveted door that opened up opportunities for university and employment in many fields. Whole families braced themselves for this particular year, especially for exam time. The stress was palpable in many students and conveyed to their parents.

I had never seen anything like it and could not relate to the serious faces and hushed tones if I visited during this period. There was so much riding on passing matric that many children became anxious and depressed, fearing failure. A South African friend recently told me that she felt pressure about passing matric several years before she even had to sit it.

As the months went by, I noticed that Eli, aged ten, had become anxious about increasing the percentage of his test results at primary school. In New Zealand, his results were marked as excellent, good, average, or poor. In contrast, his South African teachers graded him in percentages for each subject. I felt concerned when he spoke intently about improving his 84 percent mark in maths. It was strange to me that young children like him were feeling so much pressure especially when his grades were high in each subject. I could not understand the need for this intense focus on academic results at primary school. Surely creativity, relationship and communication skills, and good character were equally, if not more, essential qualities.

Just before the Counselling School began, I heard of a tragic situation as it was unfolding. A black headmaster brought one hundred children aged ten to seventeen years old to Muizenberg to attend a multi-racial boarding school. They had travelled a long distance by bus from Soweto township, near Johannesburg, but unfortunately the headmaster was a con artist. He had pocketed R 300,000 from parents who had limited funds but wanted the best for their children. Sadly, when they arrived in Muizenberg, he dumped them into two buildings without beds, blankets, or food and promptly disappeared with all the school fees.

Some YWAM leaders heard about their situation and encouraged us to help the children. Soon afterwards, some local schools also got involved. Unfortunately, the children's parents were far away, and most couldn't afford transport costs to get them back home. A few days later I met three mothers who had made the long bus trip down to assess the situation and had decided the sixty girls needed to be moved immediately.

The mothers had arranged temporary accommodation elsewhere but needed transport. I quickly checked to see if any base vehicles were available, but they weren't. As I walked home, I was crying in frustration at the plight of these vulnerable people and asked God to make a way where there didn't seem to be any.

To my delight, a teacher drove up and said he could hire a bus for R 250 if we could help with the cost. Because I had been given some money anonymously that week, I was able to pay for the bus hire. I told the mothers a bus was available and expressed my regret that they had been conned by such an unscrupulous and heartless man.

Soon after, I watched the children file onto the bus until it was totally full. A teenage boy, McMillan, stood nearby looking disorientated and distressed. He expressed deep concern that his education had been messed up, as he had been working hard towards passing the exams with distinction.

I regularly cried as I prayed about the injustices and inequalities I saw around me. Thankfully, many people genuinely wanted significant changes in their communities and the nation, but the task still seemed overwhelming at times. In response to the endemic poverty, two YWAM ladies ran a soup kitchen and a health clinic in one area. My British friend Polly planned to work among Zulu people up north, where she would be involved in a literacy programme.

It was fascinating watching as God put different desires in people's hearts. Each person was uniquely suited to work among a particular group. Some were drawn to minister to children, others to elderly, youth, drug addicts, or refugees. I discovered that our individual callings gave us the focus and passion we needed as we served God. From this, faith and courage grew when we stepped out to obey Him.

Sports day at Muizenberg Primary: First place, Eli!

CHAPTER 14

Counselling School

Once again, Joshua, Eli, and I attended school each day. I might not have been wearing a uniform like them, but I too sat at a desk, took notes during lectures, and finished my day with homework!

I was delighted to see some of my DTS classmates at my school, plus several newcomers. Altogether, there were several nations represented in our small group. We took turns introducing ourselves. Roberto was Italian; Holger, German; Ida, Norwegian; Tom, American; and I was the lady from "Down Under." We all had a similar goal of gaining valuable insights and becoming more skilled as we attended lectures by psychologists and other specialists. The format was the same as the DTS: three months of lectures, followed by a five-week outreach that Hugh, our school leader, would arrange.

Each student would be placed in different ministries or counselling clinics to gain practical experience.

Ida was the first person I had met from Norway, so I was eager to befriend her and learn why she had chosen to study at YWAM Muizenberg. It all began for her as a teenager when she heard about Nelson Mandela and South Africa on the news. I remembered seeing similar coverage in New Zealand. Awareness of the plight of millions due to apartheid laws led both our nations to boycott South Africa. The oppressed peoples' plights moved Ida's heart, especially Nelson Mandela's situation. So, over the next three years, while she worked in Oslo as a Kindergarten teacher, she focused on saving for a trip to Africa.

Ida Tobiassen.

When Ida's DTS teacher asked what her dream was, she replied, "Africa." After the DTS, she moved back to Oslo to continue working. Then a year later, a friend asked Ida to be a youth leader at a conference where she met Michael Cassidy, the leader of Africa Enterprise. After Ida spoke with him, Michael prayed for her. Sometime late when Ida was searching for YWAM Counselling Schools she discovered one in Muizenberg. Ida applied and was accepted. When we shared our expectations for the school, Ida told us she wanted to be equipped as a counsellor at her church. However, she was also expecting God to meet with her and bring greater freedom into her life.

I was fascinated by Ida's clear goals at the ripe old age of twenty-three. At thirty-seven, I was still wondering what my path was. My focus changed weekly after listening to each guest speaker. I could imagine myself involved in each of the different ministries they described. (I hadn't learnt yet that as a visionary and pioneer I quickly became excited by new opportunities and experiences.)

One of the highlights during the course was choosing specific books from the compulsory reading list. This was an absolute joy, as I am an avid reader but rarely had time to indulge before. It felt marvellous to quickly gain an understanding of a new topic that dedicated authors had spent a lifetime learning. With great skill, they managed to squeeze a brief but in-depth overview of their subject into a few chapters. I benefited enormously from their expertise but didn't realise how life-changing some of the books would be as I was repeatedly confronted with uncomfortable truths about myself.

While reading the first book (title forgotten), I saw with stark reality that I had felt short-changed in life. This was mainly due to my childhood struggles and then years of raising my sons alone with very little support or finance from their fathers. The daily pressures had been relentless and exhausting at times.

A second insight came from my trust being broken often throughout my life. Growing up, so much was "swept under the carpet" to maintain peace instead of discussing and addressing situations. Later, my husband was often absent, enjoying weekend parties, girlfriends, and drug-taking. Sadly, his behaviour added to my trust issues. As a result, I desperately needed people to be honest and not give me wrong expectations.

However, this was unrealistic, given I was in a pioneering situation where school leaders and staff were also finding their own way. It took a while to realise that when someone announced they would do XYZ, it wasn't a certainty but an idea that might or might not be implemented. Before I realised this, I had felt let down, especially when I was looking forward to something happening then, as the weeks went by, it wasn't mentioned again. After reading the first book, I discussed this issue with the school staff. They listened and prayed with me, knowing I felt vulnerable as I saw an area of unrealistic expectations in my life for the first time.

Another insight was when God exposed where "my strength" lay. I had prided myself on being a strong person who kept her word. I had lived life in my own strength instead of accepting my limitations and weaknesses and drawing my strength from God. This insight was shocking to me. For weeks afterwards, I was a bit dazed while I processed this revelation.

Just as I was coming to terms with how much I had relied on my own abilities and strength, I was struck by another truth. A lecture on guilt highlighted how I had been "overcompensating" with the boys for years because they lacked a father. Now I was doing it even more, because I had moved them away from everything familiar to a strange new land.

The motivation for much of what I was doing was guilt. I felt guilty that the boys didn't have a father in their lives, regret that I hadn't always made the wisest of choices, and increased guilt because I had brought them to Africa. In addition, because life had become increasingly challenging for the boys when we arrived, they were often lonely or unhappy. Therefore, I constantly felt compelled to do something to improve their situation. After all, it was my fault they were here.

During a ministry time to address these issues, Hugh explained that I had not enjoyed a carefree childhood, because I had taken on the responsible role of caring for my younger siblings. This role caused me a lot of anxiety, as I didn't have enough experience or wisdom to handle or even process the difficulties we faced. He suggested I read up on "parental inversion" to understand better how I had become like a parent at an early age.

Growing up in a tense, unpredictable environment, I had longed for someone to address the problems and bring an end to the constant tension and unhappiness. Because this didn't ever happen, I'd lived with a great deal of frustration and told my young self that I was on my own. I had believed that I needed to find answers to every problem I encountered. This wrong belief created more stress and anxiety.

By the fourth week of lectures, I felt vulnerable, exposed, and shaky due to the intensity of each discovery and the emotions that followed. It felt like I was unravelling a bit more each week. The strong, competent, full-of-faith Christine seemed to be dissolving right before my eyes. Finding somewhere to hide was looking more attractive by the day, but unfortunately that was not an option.

I needed to trust God when these hidden areas were being revealed, as they had to be dealt with. God was committed to freeing me from the damage of my past, so I needed to keep co-operating with Him. Once again, I made an appointment for counselling, after which I felt a sense of liberation and healing. Initially, I was concerned that I would feel belittled or condemned, but the opposite was true, as the staff wanted us to be freed of our issues.

It was great to have personal ministry times where I got in touch with how I saw life and the role I had embraced, and gradually came to understand how I dealt with problems. Naturally, it was also an emotional experience. I often cried and felt drained afterwards. After one such session, Hugh gave me a fatherly hug. I found this healing, as I viewed him as a safe, caring man.

"Uncle" Ron, an elder on the base, suggested I do a study on peace. Acknowledging that my life had been full of turmoil and stress, it made sense to study the opposite. His wife, "Aunty" May, read some verses from 2 Corinthians 1 about suffering and being comforted by Jesus. Ron and May were a gentle, kind, and wise elderly couple.

Aunty May told me, "Chris, you need to draw on God more and not continually give out." In her mind, she saw a picture of an empty tank with the red warning light on. She continued, "It's time to build up your own tank." It was a simple analogy that I could relate to. Then she spoke some profound words I've never forgotten. "You need to speak out forgiveness to your parents for not being able to give you what you needed and for what happened. Chris, parents are just little children who grow up and become parents."

Wow, what a powerful statement! I began to ponder Mum's history. She was born in Sydney to adoring parents, then lost her mother aged four. She lived with various families while her father was at sea. Finally, aged eight, Mum's father brought her to New Zealand, where she was moved among relatives before settling into a Catholic boarding school. Sadly, her father died suddenly of heart problems when she was twelve. Growing up, Mum's dream would have been to marry a kind, supportive, loving man like her father and create a happy family together.

Unfortunately, she married a volatile sailor who was often away from home. This meant Mum had to cope alone, doing the best she could without any family support. My father, his three brothers, and his little sister grew up while their father was away at sea for months then was absent for six years during World War II. The boys were independent teenagers when he returned. My dad followed in the footsteps of his father, uncles, and brothers by becoming a sailor at seventeen. A ship was a well-run, male-dominated environment. No wonder Dad became restless when he was at home for longer than a couple of weeks.

Dad's frequent absences meant we lived two different lives growing up. Life was relaxed and fun when Dad was away but tense and unpleasant once he returned. He was strict and controlling, prone to sudden angry outbursts. These outbursts were generally triggered when the television was too loud, or we hadn't done the dishes. It was a relief for us all when he packed his kit bag and left for another voyage.

As I pondered my parents' imperfect lives, I was able to speak forgiveness to them, releasing them from my judgments and the anger I had carried deep within my soul for years. The feeling of lightness I experienced afterwards was wonderful. However, as the weeks progressed, instead of being my usually bubbly self who enjoyed people's company, I became withdrawn and increasingly felt out of touch with myself. I was confused, as I didn't understand the reason for this change.

When I shared my internal dilemma with Ida, my Norwegian friend, she surprised me by announcing, "Chris, you're going through an identity crisis." Bingo! She had pinpointed the heart of the matter. So much had changed that I felt like I didn't know myself anymore. I had a picture of a small, quiet person living inside a large building with many noisy, energetic people. The enthusiastic, extroverted Christine was nowhere to be seen; in her place was a passive, disinterested, touchy introvert. I felt hopeless and unsure how to help myself, but my faithful Heavenly Father was busy behind the scenes. Werner May, a psychologist, was the next lecturer. During the week, I made an appointment and shared with him how I felt broken, empty, and out of touch with God and people. He listened, then began to pray.

As Werner prayed, he saw a picture of a vase with a hole in the bottom. He prayed for God to seal it and for the Holy Spirit to refill me with His love and peace. Werner observed that I probably didn't realise I was still friendly and outgoing, but because of the peace that was now in my life, I felt very quiet. Peace was a new sensation! Werner explained that excitement had energised me previously, but now it was not my primary motivator.

Werner's explanation about this new sense of peace was unexpected but fascinating. I had never lived with an ongoing deep sense of peace before, so I hadn't recognised it. He said, "God is doing a deep work in you, so relax. You are still the same warm, bubbly person, but you relate differently to people now. You will find people will relate to you differently also." This quieter version of me had caused a deep sense of disorientation, but thankfully Werner assured me the outgoing quality of my persona had not changed. I just needed time to process all I had been through and get used to having a more peaceful and calm inner world. That sounded good to me!

Soon after my ministry time with Werner, I had a memorable experience. Our school had combined with the School of Evangelism for a time of worship. While I was focusing on how lonely and alone I felt, a thought popped into my mind. "Why don't you ask me to come in?" I knew this was God showing me what I needed to do. The truth was that He had always been with me, but somehow I had forgotten to ask Him about my situation. This was the obvious answer. I quickly prayed, "Please come into my heart and life afresh." God's reassuring presence flowed over me, and I felt the loneliness go.

Focusing on my loving Father, I said, "Now that I've given you more room in my heart, I want to talk to you about everything, friend to friend." Using my imagination, I saw myself and God sitting in large, comfy armchairs while I told him what had been happening recently. His gaze was loving and brought me great comfort.

After that, I realised I needed to spend more time chatting with and listening to God and not getting so caught up in the busyness of each day. For years I had focused on hearing from God, rushing off to obey, then returning to report back to Him. As I reflected on this, I saw Him take my face in His hands, lean forward, and hug me. Reassurance of His love and acceptance flooded my soul. The verse from Revelations 3:20 came to mind: "Behold I stand at the door and knock. If anyone hears my voice and opens the door, I will come in to him and eat with him, and he with me." I said, "Jesus, I need to relate to you more naturally and share all of my life with you, not just the big stuff but all the daily details as well." This perspective felt like a brand-new beginning for me. I was very grateful for this fresh encounter with the One who knew me best.

DTS graduation dinner.

CHAPTER 15

Boundaries

Before taking the counselling course, I had no idea how much I would be applying the new truths I learnt to my own life. Believing I was well able to counsel others, it came as a shock each week when another issue was highlighted. I felt embarrassed at first, but soon realised we were all in the same boat. God was stripping off the baggage of our pasts. Of course, being the eldest student and a parent, I probably had many more layers than the younger students.

One of my favourite weeks was when Hugh taught us from a manual called Apples of Gold. It was a huge eye-opener that changed how I responded to people, especially when I wanted to help solve their problems. I learnt that when someone shared a problem, it was essential to take time to identify two key aspects:

(1) what was the actual problem? and (2) whose problem was it? By doing this, I could clarify whose responsibility the problem was.

Before learning this skill, I enthusiastically took others' problems on board and enjoyed finding solutions for them. However, this teaching helped me recognise that I was easily manipulated, even by my young sons! If, for example, they hadn't completed a project or homework on time and knew they could be in trouble with their teacher, I would quickly help them. After attending a few lectures, I realised I was actually protecting the boys from the consequences of poor choices like watching television or playing with others when they should have been working on their projects. I discovered that children learn to make responsible decisions by owning their own problems instead of having adults intervene on their behalf. Regularly solving a child's issues enables unwise behaviour. I had often felt pressured to help the boys. But now I could apply my new skills to their situations and to anyone else who came for counselling. Naturally, I was eager to put this new method into practice.

The following day when I was asked for help by a person with a recurring situation, I quietly assessed their request and thought, "Let's identify the problem. What is it exactly?" After answering that, I asked myself the second question, "Whose problem is it?" And, of course, it was theirs, not mine. Identifying this made it much easier for me to listen without taking ownership of their problem. Instead, I encouraged them to ask God to help them find a solution. This method was easy, helpful, and straightforward. It also provided clarity and freed me from becoming weighed down when I had my own situations to deal with.

For years, I'd thought I was showing concern when I "solved" people's problems, including my sons'. At an early age, my sons had learnt to keep pressuring me if I was reluctant to do something they wanted. Because, eventually, I would capitulate just to gain some peace.

It was a shock to learn that attempting to solve someone else's problems was disrespectful; I was unknowingly telling them they could not handle their situations, but I could. I was horrified at that thought, as it smacked of pride. Meanwhile, I gained some understanding about what had been motivating my behaviour. When listening to a person describing their difficult problems, I often became anxious for them so I would suggest a solution.

Having spent most of my adult life as a single parent, I had been forced to handle a wide range of challenges on my own. This was stressful but unavoidable. Over time I had developed a habit of quickly dealing with everything myself rather than looking to others for help.

The lesson on manipulation gave me many valuable insights and a determination to stop "rescuing" people. Of course, as I enthusiastically applied the principles with my boys, they were not impressed. But instead of feeling weighed down and harassed, I now felt buoyant and empowered. However, it wasn't long before Eli let me know what he thought of my newly acquired skills. With a sad expression, he lamented, "I wish you hadn't done this course, 'cos we can't make you change your mind anymore." I was amazed at his self-awareness.

Life was much easier for me after the valuable lesson on not owning others' problems. I saw clearly that people often became dependent on whoever was offering solutions instead of asking God for His intervention and wisdom. This was a common trap.

A favourite book on my compulsory reading list was *Inside Out* by Dr. Larry Crabb, a renowned psychotherapist. He explained that, for most of us, arranging our own comfort was our top priority. This is why we look to people to meet our needs. When we feel hurt, we want it to end quickly and develop self-defence systems as a way to protect ourselves. But only God can satisfy the deepest longings of our hearts, so we need to take our disappointments and pain to Him.

Larry described our dilemma of needing to be loved while acknowledging that relationships can be painful.

The truth is, God loves us deeply. However, He does not give instant relief or act immediately, and this can cause us to doubt Him.

I thought back to 1980 when God gave me a vision revealing that my future would be in Africa. I immediately applied for a passport and approached missions organisations to let them know I was called and willing to go. However, even though I was keen to obey, I experienced ten long, frustrating years where every door I knocked on slammed shut.

Living with this uncomfortable calling to missions in Africa, while being rejected by every organisation I applied to, was incredibly confusing and frustrating. At times, I wondered if God was even concerned that His calling constantly made me restless and sometimes an object of ridicule.

Then I read about Joseph in the Old Testament. He went through a similar situation where he received a vision that didn't seem to be coming to pass for many long and painful years. Larry Crabb stated that, while we hope for swift intervention during tough times, God can't be controlled by us, our emotions, or our demanding words.

When problems drag on, we sometimes conclude God is not managing our situation very well, so we try to "help" him. Unfortunately, this thinking usually complicates things and creates new problems. Because we often lack self-awareness about our thoughts and behaviour, God uses the Holy Spirit, His Word, and people we feel safe with to give us insights and feedback.

I identified with the cycle of disappointment leading to isolation, defensiveness, and a fear of being hurt again. When I felt disappointed by God, I often became anxious and demanding. This was an uncomfortable picture, but one I had to acknowledge in order to end the lonely cycle. God definitely loved me, had sent his Son to die for me, and had made many promises I'd highlighted throughout my Bible. I needed to focus on His promises instead of becoming impatient when things didn't work out quickly enough for my liking. Being disappointed with God created distrust, which robbed me of peace and the assurance of His many promises. Also, being disappointed in people prevented me from enjoying my friends and family. After all, these were special people who brought kindness, love, and fun into my life.

Larry Crabb recommended developing rich relation-ships with people who dared to give honest feedback after listening to what was troubling us. Honest feed-back was the most helpful tool in assisting us to grow. I felt fortunate because I was experiencing this during each counselling session. The honest feedback from lecturers and staff gave me a new perspective. Naturally, the feedback process was not always comfortable, but it helped free me from negative cycles of behaviour and thinking. I felt grateful to God for making this time possible. It was a wonderful gift.

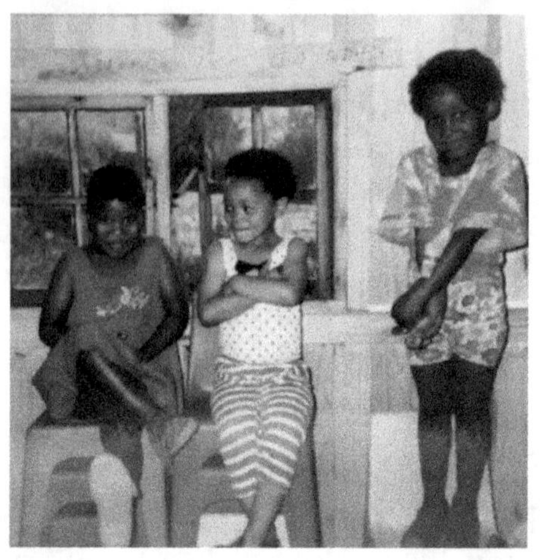

Above and right:
Adorable local children.

CHAPTER 16

Ramona

Part way through the course, one hundred staff and students went on a weekend outreach to a needy local area. We interacted with the families there and helped out where we could. A pretty little girl with a massive mop of unruly curly hair, Ramona, attached herself to me and insisted I take her back to my home. She wore grubby, torn clothes and desperately needed a bath. As she was constantly scratching her head, I could tell a large infestation of head lice had taken up residence in her beautiful curls and on her scalp.

On Sunday, Ramona clung to me when we were saying goodbye, pleading to come back to Muizenberg. I was willing, as I could see she was not being looked after very well, but the reality was I only had a small room and wasn't sure of the staff's reaction if I took her to Surf

Inn. However, I couldn't leave her, especially when she explained her mother had abandoned the family a few weeks before. To my surprise, when I offered to take Ramona, her father readily agreed. He explained he was busy caring for his 14-month-old son, Yalzado. Without employment or an income, they were all suffering and had been reduced to living in a small shack near the beach.

I could see the trauma of being abandoned and not getting enough to eat on Ramona's face. Her eyes were sad, reflecting the pain from all the trauma she had experienced in her short life. So I brought the delightful little girl back with me and spent an hour removing the multitude of lice from her thick curls. Of course, some lice had migrated to me while I was cuddling her, so before long I was also scratching my scalp furiously. Sometimes love has unexpected costs!

Ramona.

Ramona enjoyed a long, warm shower while trying the fragrant hair shampoo and body wash, then snuggled up in bed with me. She was an adorable, affectionate child who became quite animated once she knew she wasn't going back to the shack. Josh and Eli were a bit startled to see a little girl snuggled up in my bed, but they were used to various people living with us in New Zealand, so they quickly accepted Ramona.

As I had lectures and couldn't leave her alone, I took her with me on Monday morning. She sat beside me looking very happy. Hugh, our school leader, observed the little addition to our class but, to his credit, didn't make any negative comments.

The following weekend when I took Ramona home to her father, my heart broke at the sight of their 'home'. It was an old metal tool shed on an empty site. Inside was bleak; there was no covering over the dirt floor, no table, chairs, beds, or toys. The shed was barren and cold. No wonder Ramona had begged me not to leave her in this squalid environment.

Her dad could not work because he took care of Yalzado, a happy, trusting little boy who constantly smiled, oblivious to the abject poverty they lived in. At first, some students wondered if I had done the right thing bringing Ramona to Surf Inn with all its comforts and a vastly different standard of living. But there was no way I could leave this beautiful, loving child who was grieving for her mother to live in a cold, barren tool shed. Before long, lovely little Ramona had won her way into many people's hearts. I regularly saw her cuddled up in bed with my ex-roommate Judy or sitting on someone's knee.

The staff and students enjoyed having Ramona with us, and soon her little brother Yalzado joined her on weekends. A young staff member, Michelle, adored him and gladly gave up her weekends to care for him. Because the students obviously cared for the children, I suggested we have a collection to buy them some essentials. Both children needed basic clothing, and Yalzado also needed nappies, as he only had four cloth ones.

To my delight, the students gave generously. The following day, Ramona and I caught a train to Fish Hoek, enjoying the sea views along the coastline. From our carriage, we watched seals weaving in and out of the waves. The antics of these surfing seals made us smile. I had recently been told that Orca whales would arrive in our bay to give birth to their young as the weather warmed up. I looked forward to seeing these impressive creatures close up.

In the children's clothing section, I began my search for some basic clothes for Ramona. Meanwhile, she headed off to the shoe department. After choosing leggings, undies, singlets, and tops, I joined her as I planned to buy her some sturdy casual shoes. However, Ramona had her heart set on a pair of "Sunday school" shoes. She was clutching a pair of black patent leather shoes with a cute bow. They were totally inappropriate for where she lived but I knew the chances of her ever owning a similar pair would be slim. So to squeals of delight, I added them to the growing pile of clothes and nappies. Once I paid for the shoes, she quickly put them on and handed me her old scruffy pair. Ramona was ecstatic to be wearing such pretty, shiny shoes. I enjoyed watching her looking at them and smiling with delight on the train ride home.

When we arrived at Surf Inn, she began modelling all her new gear, much to everyone's amusement. Ramona pranced up and down the long hallway in her shiny new Sunday school shoes as if she was on a catwalk. We all enjoyed her uninhibited performance.

For three weekends, Ramona and Yalzado came to stay. But the next weekend when Michelle and I went out to the shed, they were gone. We both felt a deep sense of loss and concern for these precious little children who had crossed our path and won so many hearts. All we could do was to pray for protection for them. A few months later, we heard that Ramona and Yalzado were living with their mother. She had found employment that enabled her to provide for them. We were all relieved that Ramona's mother had returned to the shack and taken the children to a better environment. Thank you, God, for answering our prayers.

When you see hundreds of thousands of people living in abject poverty with huts made from plastic, cardboard, and bits of metal, your appreciation for the simple things of life becomes heightened. I became grateful for a roof that didn't leak, an indoor flush toilet, a shower with hot water, a comfortable bed, and three meals a day. I had learned that these ordinary things that I had taken for granted all my life were actually luxuries to many people worldwide. I now wanted to share the blessings I had taken for granted.

The boys were also impacted by the plight of people around us. When Eli and I were travelling to Capetown by train, a disabled man came into our carriage. He looked unkempt and dejected. I watched as Eli promptly took his pocket money and gave it to him. This man's plight had touched my ten-year-old son's heart. I was proud of him for responding with compassion. So many people were suffering and in desperate need of assistance, and we couldn't help but be moved by their situations. The government in New Zealand provided a generous disability allowance and subsidised housing for those on a lower income, but here they received a pittance.

After six months in South Africa and a few outreaches, I had a special love for coloured folk. I believed the little Ramonas and Yalzados of this world deserved to live in a warm home with adequate food and an opportunity for a good education, especially as God placed a dream in every child's heart that needed to be nurtured and encouraged as they grew older.

Eli turned eleven towards the end of July and celebrated with an enormous, yummy chocolate cake. It was a Surf Inn special, designed to give over seventy people a slice. After years of having celebrations at home surrounded by family and close friends, Eli was now part of a broad international group heartily singing happy birthday in English and Afrikaans. This was his new family.

Meanwhile, I was preparing for final exams, which would bring our lecture phase to an end. We were all keen to hear from Hugh about where our placements would be. I had struggled with sitting at a desk for weeks on end. I preferred to be doing something practical, but it had been necessary. After writing my exams, I was delighted to discover that I had passed with an 'A' grade. This course had hugely impacted my life, and now I was keen to put some of the new lessons and skills into practice. Listening to the teachers, I had observed that deep trust and dependence on God, dedication, commitment, and sheer hard work were all keys to being effective in ministry.

My desire was to be involved in family counselling in a community setting where I could begin to earn some money to supplement our sporadic support. However, when I visited Home Affairs in Cape Town to renew my student's visa, I was informed that I was not allowed to officially be employed, This was due to the high unemployment rate and the policy of employing local citizens before foreigners. This limitation dashed my hopes of any additional finances. Instead, I accepted that we were totally dependent on God's provision long-term.

Often, I marvelled at the timing of a letter or postcard that arrived when I felt drained, overwhelmed, or discouraged. Reading words of love and encouragement boosted me and reminded me of the many people praying for us. These unexpected blessings in the mail also reminded me God knew how I was feeling and had prompted someone to write an uplifting message to me. As a result, I was increasingly aware of needing the support of my family and friends in our journey into the unknown.

The reality was that it sometimes became lonely in our mission's environment. New friends regularly departed after their courses. There seemed to be a revolving population every three months. A long-term member of staff told me she had stopped making new friends, as she was tired of bonding with people only to see them leave a few months later. Pondering her statement, I decided I would keep reaching out and enjoy friendships, however brief they were.

CHAPTER 17

Messy Ending

After the lecture phase ended, my fellow students and I waited to be placed with the different organisations Hugh had contacted. So far, three students were going up north to a ministry focused on rehabilitation for alcoholics. Another girl would work in Cape Town with an organisation that helped abused children.

The boisterous, loud School of Evangelism students left on their outreach, and suddenly Surf Inn became quieter. Ten students from my school and some from the School of Frontier Missions remained, plus the boys and me.

Rob and Marianne were heading up a team to Malawi but needed to sort out transport first. Eventually, they found a fifty-year-old Land Rover that Rob, a mechanic, was confident he could coax to haul seven adults and three children for several thousand miles.

By now, the atmosphere in Surf Inn had become strained and tense again. Everyone was tired after three months of classes, assignments, work duties, and living with over seventy people. We all longed for a few days to sleep in, take long walks on the beach, or visit friends. Knowing we were about to begin a challenging new outreach phase, most of us looked forward to a week of relaxation.

I had a cold and was feeling lethargic, so I spent most of my spare time in my room once the boys had left for school. While having a quick meal downstairs one lunchtime, I became aware of mounting frustration and anger among the students. I wasn't sure if this was due to the constant pressure of not knowing which doors would open or shut, facing continuous money worries, or in response to how they were being spoken to. I understood some of the pressures, especially not knowing when finance would arrive or how much it would be. There was no doubt we were all missing Francois and his team's gentle, calm presence. Francois often sat with a coffee in the dining room surrounded by young people from both schools, chatting and laughing as they teased each other. The place felt empty and lonely once they all departed.

However, my role was to support the boys while they went through their own challenges and adjustments. It was crucial to stay positive and confident, even though I didn't know where my placement would be, what hours I would be working, or where we would move to in the future.

By the end of the Counselling School, it was early September. We had lived in South Africa for nine months, had moved three times already, and lived among a large group of constantly changing people. We hadn't had a holiday or even a weekend away together during those nine months. A break felt long overdue. There hadn't been an opportunity to quietly process things on my own or even do sightseeing as a family. I kept hearing about fabulous tourist attractions like Kruger National Park and Addo Elephant Park but had neither the time nor money to visit them.

At least with my placement, I would be away from Surf Inn each day, learning counselling skills and meeting different people. I was looking forward to this new season. At the start of my week off, a Dutch couple arrived at Surf Inn with their children. Like the Vermeys and me, they had given up everything and arrived in Muizenberg to begin Missions training. But just like the Vermeys, their school leader was not expecting them, so nothing had been prepared for them. I knew they had arrived full of anticipation and hope for this new phase in their lives and was dismayed to see the shock and confusion on their faces when they discovered suitable rooms were not ready. Obviously, another cross-cultural communication mix-up had occurred, leaving the family distressed and the manageress perplexed.

I watched the new arrivals struggle to process and cope with what they had just been told and was surprised at how deeply their situation impacted me emotionally. The Vermeys and I understood the enormity of what had taken place for them to make it to South Africa. However, once in South Africa, we all relied on the experienced base staff and school leaders to ease our entry into this complex, multi-layered nation.

Later that day, as I was walking past the laundry, a young staff member, Colette, called out to me and asked how I was doing. To my surprise, I began crying while telling her how difficult I was finding life in Surf Inn. For some time, I had been praying for a flat to move into so I could rebuild our family unit. I needed somewhere away from all the tensions and upsets of community living. After Collette hugged me, I headed upstairs to my snug little room. Then, a few minutes later, I was called to the public phone.

To my surprise, I heard the base director's wife asking how I was. I can't remember what I replied. I didn't know her well but guessed she was responding to a call from Colette, with whom I had shared my heart. After a few minutes of awkwardly trying to decide what I should say to her, she told me they cared and were sending someone over to see me. I was now feeling horribly uncomfortable and confused. A simple, honest conversation with one person seemed to have taken on a life of its own.

The director's wife had asked Shelby, an American lady whom I didn't know well, to come and see me. Feeling vulnerable and nervous, I wondered what she would say. A short time later, I was told that Shelby had been delayed, as my school leader had asked her to visit him first. Oh no! A fourth person was getting involved! I sat in my room for a long time, squirming and feeling sick inside. I didn't have a good feeling about this visit.

Eventually, Shelby arrived. Having prayed for wisdom, I decided to be honest with her about the tense environment in Surf Inn. She listened, then told me in a stern voice that I was being critical, and said she was "frightened by my expectations of YWAM," which were not realistic!

Feeling great shame, I listened as Shelby stressed that I was not to agonise in public but rather pray in private. When I noticed or sensed things, I was to pray and not discuss them. After outlining some "realities" I seemed to have been unaware of, Shelby concluded that I needed to raise financial support, as this would help me feel less "insecure." Her closing remark was, "A woman needs a home." She ended our time together with a prayer.

By the time Shelby left, I was drowning in shame. I was stunned and wished the floor had opened up to swallow me. Could I really have been so ignorant and out of touch with what I was coming to? A great sense of having messed up badly descended on me. For some time, I sat in my room, shaken, feeling inadequate and thoroughly told off. Knowing how I was viewed made me reluctant to face anyone, but I needed to compose myself for the boys who were about to arrive home.

The following day I cried out to God to rescue me and get us out of Surf Inn. I pleaded with Him using verses based on Psalm 40: "God, hear my cry, lift me out of the pit, set my feet on a rock, and give me a firm place to stand. Lord, come quickly to help me. You are my help and deliverer." I focused on God's promises in this crisis. I desperately needed some respite from all the tension.

Soon afterwards, my leader Hugh visited me with what I hoped would be good news. Instead, he surprised me by explaining that my outreach had fallen through. Before I could grasp the full impact of not being able to fulfil my course requirements, Hugh asked me what I was going to do.

I was so stunned at this unexpected turn of events that I couldn't reply. Obviously, I didn't know what I would do, as I had expected to be training in a counselling clinic for the next three months. Trying hard to adjust to this blow, I was unprepared for what followed. He explained that we would have to leave Surf Inn in three days, as new students were arriving.

Hugh asked if I had thought about living at Wavecrest. "Of course not," I thought. It was a disgusting old building that the council was planning to demolish. But first, after kicking out all the homeless people who had been squatting there, they had offered it to YWAM on a monthly basis. I couldn't imagine anyone wanting to live in the enormous, filthy building, let alone me and the boys.

The decrepit old place was being broken into at night by alcoholics and vandals, who were stealing copper pipes and drinking there. I was staggered at the possibility of taking the boys into such a run-down, dangerous situation. However, Hugh assured me that the staff and students would help clear out the worst of the mess, including huge amounts of pigeon poop. Hundreds of pigeons lived under the roof, causing smelly poop to run down the bedroom walls where they had separated from the ceiling. Hugh assured me a work party would help with the clean-up, but I needed to tackle the mess as best I could until that was organised.

I was horrified at the prospect of us living in Wavecrest, but because my cold had turned into flu, my foggy mind was not working efficiently. I kept silent while Hugh shared more details.

The boys and I could live at Wavecrest for R 200 a month per bedroom and R 120 per person for meals. However, we would need to have meals at Surf Inn, as Wavecrest had no functioning kitchen or working showers. I knew living there would be humiliating and distressing for the boys. Another concern was that the front door didn't have a proper lock. That felt scary, but apparently the base maintenance guy would fix the lock, and a male student would move in when we did.

While Hugh was waiting for my answer, he offered to counsel me in a few weeks' time when he returned from a family holiday. I am sure he could see how overwhelmed I was. He commented that I needed to have some family time after such a busy nine months and suggested that I help to decorate Wavecrest for a few weeks. I was dazed. It was a lot of unpleasant news to absorb and process in one go.

Before leaving, Hugh said he'd been at an emergency meeting all morning with base leaders because of a blow-up at Surf Inn last night. When students who were tired and stressed were informed that they needed to work each day to cover the cost of their accommodation and food, they became angry and vocal. The reality was that furniture needed moving and maintenance jobs required attention. In addition, the public areas and bedrooms needed to be cleaned, and students had to participate in kitchen duties if they wanted regular meals. Some frustrated students had erupted verbally on hearing this unwelcome information. Hugh was asked to mediate. It had obviously been a long morning for him before he even spoke with me.

After Hugh delivered his news, I felt shocked and numb. I wanted to curl up in a foetal position while someone else came up with a speedy plan to end this nightmare. But the reality was that I didn't have the luxury of switching off for a few days while I slept and recovered from the flu. I needed to be brave and decisive, as two young lads depended on me to stay strong and make wise decisions on their behalf.

My lack of knowledge about how the world of missions operated meant I had not prepared financially by raising sufficient monthly support before leaving New Zealand. My ignorance and lack of experience had caused this embarrassing and frightening situation. Worst of all, I felt I had become a burden to the base.

I realised it would have been unpleasant for Hugh to give me such a lot of negative news; he knew I believed God had called me to Africa long term and that I'd been preparing for ten years. Hugh had a kind, fatherly heart and had been a fantastic support to me throughout the school.

Still, I felt foolish and naive to have believed God would automatically supply all our needs just because I had obeyed him by giving everything up and moving to Africa. It was now apparent that I should have focused on raising a solid support base among my friends and family while still in New Zealand. But no one had spoken to me about this aspect. Some training or information on this crucial area of missions before coming to YWAM would have made a considerable difference and lessened the stress and confusion I was now facing. Instead, I was tired, discouraged, overwhelmed, broke, and battling nasty flu. All I could do was murmur, "Please help me, God," before falling asleep. I didn't even have the energy to cry!

The next day, I was asked to help set up rooms for the new schools that were starting in three days. One of the helpers confided she was feeling weary and was wanting to prepare for a friend's wedding on Saturday. She, too, was struggling, but together we lifted, carried, and cleaned until the job was done.

An hour later Josh arrived back from school. He came straight to my room, distressed at his low science mark on his school report. Thankfully he had achieved good results in the other subjects. As we chatted, it became clear he had several other things on his mind that were weighing him down. His birthday was in a week, but with Charlie and his friends in the School of Evangelism away, he felt that he wouldn't have a proper celebration. Josh was missing them and also having problems with someone at school. I listened quietly, then shared my thoughts before suggesting we pray. Overall, he was feeling alone and overwhelmed with life's demands. We had a cuddle, then he fell asleep on my bed. It was clear I needed to build up our fragile family unit.

The deadline for moving from Surf Inn was Thursday afternoon. I knew I couldn't do this alone and without transport. Another problem was that after we moved, our rooms would need to be thoroughly cleaned in readiness for the incoming students. Being so sick, I wasn't sure how all this would happen. But God had a plan!

Little cuties.

CHAPTER 18

Wavecrest

Three angels came to my rescue on the day of the big move. Rob and Marianne had enlisted the help of Roberto from the Counselling School. Together they managed to pack all our belongings as well as two single beds into a van.

When the van arrived, Rob and Roberto carried the cases and boxes upstairs while Marianne and I unpacked some essentials. She helped me with the boys' room first, then we tackled my room. I was very grateful for Marianne's help, as the flu had sapped all my energy.

We didn't have any wardrobes or drawers, so I made side tables from cardboard boxes and covered them with a cloth. The room I chose for the boys was spacious, with enormous bay windows looking out to sea.

I remembered some good advice my sister Margy had given before we left: "As soon as you move anywhere, make the beds up with the boys' duvet covers and put their favourite posters on the wall. That way, they will each have a personal space that looks familiar." She was right! After making up the boys' beds, I began putting some posters on the wall.

Everything took twice as long to do as I was still unwell. I chose a smaller room next to the boys for myself, so we could have a sense of closeness. Thankfully both bedroom doors had a working lock, which would give us a sense of safety while we slept. The boys and I would be alone, as the male student who was supposed to be moving in hadn't arrived.

The day before, Marianne had explained our situation to the manageress and asked for beds for us. The boys were given one each; unfortunately, no bed was available for me. I didn't mind this inconvenience, as my priority was the boys. However, the Vermeys were outraged at our plight of having to move into a dirty, derelict building.

I wasn't too happy about the situation either, especially as our new temporary home was two stories high and had twenty-nine bedrooms. But at least we would have our choice of bedrooms, preferably some with sturdy locks on the doors. I was looking forward to having a quiet place to recover from the shocks of that week.

Wavecrest by the sea.

There was no denying Wavecrest was a frightful place that reeked of abject poverty and pigeon poop, but unexpectedly it was to become our home. I needed to quickly create some kind of comfort for the boys before they arrived back from school.

After setting up the bedrooms, my first task was to locate an electric socket. After a quick search, I found that there were only two in the whole upstairs hall. Surprisingly they were both close to our bedrooms. This was handy, as we had no hot water available or even a stove to cook on. At least I could create a place for our appliances. First I laid a clean piece of cardboard on the floor directly in front of one socket, then I positioned a small wooden table on it for our newly acquired toaster, kettle, and other basics. I named this section of the landing "The Breakfast Bar."

When Marianne asked permission for us to eat at Surf Inn, the manageress initially refused but thankfully later had a change of heart and agreed. I didn't mind living on crackers and cheese, but the boys needed something more substantial at the end of the day. I was relieved and grateful once their meals were taken care of.

When the boys returned from school, I decided I would encourage them to think of our situation as "indoor camping." Nothing like a bit of denial to cope with overwhelming realities! I braced myself for their looks of horror once they saw the reality of this building. Although it felt like we were in a desperate situation, I couldn't let the boys know what I thought, as this would make them anxious and scared. Instead, I needed to remain strong and positive while they struggled to come to terms with what had happened to us.

Joshua was the first one home. To my surprise, he enthusiastically ran upstairs, flung his school bag onto his bed, and stood in front of the enormous bedroom windows with a look of sheer delight. It was as if he was drinking in the panoramic view of the sea. Josh was in seventh heaven at discovering he had a fabulous view of the surf conditions at all times. (Recently, he commented that being able to hear the sea every morning and night while he lay in bed was incredibly soothing for him. This experience became his favourite memory of South Africa.)

Feeling as though I'd dodged a bullet with Josh's enthusiastic response, I waited for Eli to arrive, guessing his reaction would differ from his brothers. When I heard a car door closing, I looked out the window and saw Eli getting out. I knew he was embarrassed that his school friends in the back seat had seen his grotty new "home." He looked quite apprehensive as he slowly climbed the stairs. After a cursory glance at the room, he lay on his bed, hunched up with his back to us. The shame of being dropped off here and realising we didn't have enough money to rent a flat was scary for him. What he needed was some time alone to process our downfall. I knew that words wouldn't make any difference at this stage.

However, it wasn't long before Eli joined us in creating a cardboard table to make their room more homely. To my surprise, the Portuguese lady running the hot bread shop sent over some pots, various kitchen utensils, and a set of drawers for the boys' clothes. It was a lovely gesture. The blessings continued. Lyn, a local lady about to attend the next Crossroads School, offered me a double bed and mattress. She had heard about our situation on the YWAM grapevine. Lyn promptly organised transport to deliver a bed she didn't need for

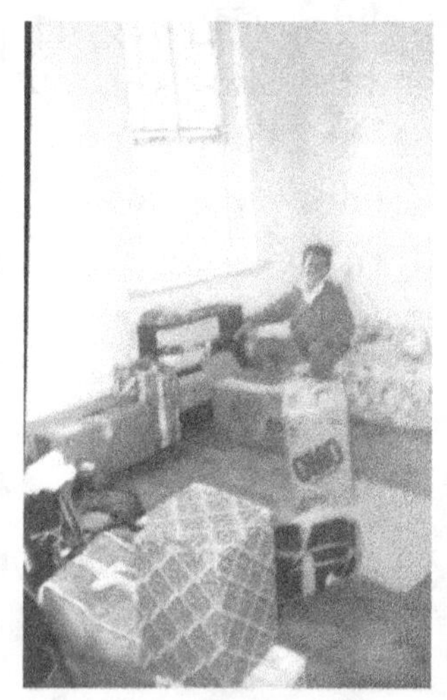

Setting up the boys' room.

the next six months. I was grateful to all the community folk who generously showed their concern for us in practical ways.

Having done what we could to decorate our rooms, I sent the boys off to Surf Inn for dinner while I went to check on the guy who was working downstairs on the front door lock. He was a retired military man who had become the base maintenance guy. I relied on his skills to sort out the lock that was not functioning correctly, because the boys and I needed protection. After taking it apart and trying a few things, he finally packed his tools away and announced that a new part was required to finish the job. Unfortunately, as it was dinner time, he had to head home. Before leaving, he looked at me with a frown. "I wouldn't let my wife stay here," he said, then walked off.

I was dumbfounded at what had just happened and stood at the entranceway in shock. Of course, he wouldn't let his wife stay here; no one would. It was a dangerous situation. But this was now our home, so I had to compose myself and get ready for the frightening prospect of sleeping in an unlocked building. Squatters and alcoholics wouldn't even need to break in to gain access; they could simply open the front door and walk in.

When the boys returned from dinner, they spent some time doing homework and exploring the old building.

Many years ago, South African and international guests would have had a fantastic holiday in Wavecrest, with close access to the beach and sea. The ground floor had several small rooms along the side walls, a kitchen at the back, and a narrow spiral staircase (previously for servants) hugging the back corner. An expansive central area had probably been the dining room or lounge. Unfortunately, the building was now a shabby old relic from a bygone era, empty except for a few hundred pigeons and us.

Before bedtime, I instructed the boys to keep their room locked all night and not come out, regardless of what they heard. Then I retreated to my room and prayed for God's protection over the three of us. I lay in bed trying to process the day's events. Even though the room was warm, my body felt cold inside and out. I have never experienced this before or since. It was as if I had been stunned. Also, I was unwell, with a sore throat and chesty cough that was not likely to improve with loads of pigeon poop and dust everywhere.

Even though I was mentally, emotionally, and physically exhausted, I couldn't sleep. I felt irresponsible for reducing the boys and myself to this level of poverty and dependence on people I lacked confidence in. Alone, I could have adapted or gone to live with Elaine, but my boys didn't deserve what was happening. I cried out to God in anguish and confusion, "What have I done?"

Our lives were unravelling, and I felt powerless to stop it. All night I lay in a state of shock, with a deep sense of abandonment. It was a relief when morning finally arrived. The boys headed to Surf Inn for a shower and breakfast before walking to school.

I was relieved that Sandra and a male student were moving in and decided their rooms would be the first ones I'd fix. Initially, I felt overwhelmed at the enormous task ahead of me, but fortunately, the base had arranged for some students to help in the afternoons. They arrived with buckets, mops, and cleaning liquid to begin making Wavecrest more habitable. Their enthusiasm and energy were great. All I had to do was show them the neediest areas; a few hours later, the place was clean and fragrant.

True to his word, the maintenance guy returned with the exact parts needed to fix the front door lock. It was a relief to feel safe again, especially as South Africa had one of the highest rates of murder and rape in the world!

When Sandra arrived, I showed her the room I had prepared and the 'breakfast bar' where the toaster and

The breakfast bar.

kettle were set up. With her company, I felt more settled. Downstairs we found a ping pong table that we set up. Over the coming weeks it provided us with some much needed fun and light-hearted competitions. I found playing with other tenants was a welcome addition to our home and a great way to relax. We didn't have a couch or television, but we had a stunning natural environment right outside our front door where we could swim, surf, or simply enjoy long walks.

On the second night, I was almost asleep when I heard a noise along the landing and a thud outside my bedroom door. I quickly sat up, ready to defend myself, but the would-be robber knocked on my door and called out, "Let me in!" It was Sandra. She had dragged her camp bed across the landing from her room to mine. As her door didn't have a lock, she felt insecure and had decided to join me. Chuckling to myself, I let her in and settled down once again. My impromptu roommate struggled to get comfortable on her narrow canvas camp bed. "There's never a dull moment here," I thought, slowly drifting off to sleep.

At 2 a.m., I was jolted awake by the front door banging shut. I quietly got up to find out who had made the noise. To my relief, it was only the second male student moving in. We had been expecting him to arrive during the day! Once again, I snuggled down and finally slept till morning.

Without curtains, the morning sun streamed in to greet us, highlighting about forty flies spinning in circles above us. Eli made short work of our unwelcome guests with fly spray. I made a hot cup of Rooibos (Red Bush) tea for Sandra and me to enjoy while we planned our day.

It was Saturday, so the boys would be out with their friends while I continued to try and make a "silk purse out of a pig's ear!" This old English expression was very apt for what was taking place at Wavecrest. The odds were against us in creating a hygienic, inviting place for incoming residents, but I had nothing else to do so tackled a different area each day. First, I created pretty pot plants for the downstairs windows, then hung donated net curtains for privacy. These simple improvements made the place look more welcoming and cared for.

During the day, many visitors came to see where we lived, bringing gifts. Kim, who assisted the manageress of Surf Inn, arrived with a china jug full of milk. I promptly put the kettle on and showed her around. It was fascinating watching people's reactions as they imagined themselves having to live here. I guessed they would return to their cosy rooms with more gratitude after their visits to Wavecrest!

One of my favourite pastimes was sitting outside on the balcony, greeting people as they walked by and watching Joshua bodysurfing. He was in the water most days with the surfing guys from YWAM. I was happy for him, as it was a source of constant pleasure after a long, hot day at school.

While looking out from the boys' window, I often spotted a group of orca whales that had travelled thousands of miles to give birth to their babies. False Bay was a safe place for them and had plenty of horse mackerel, providing them with essential protein. The adult orcas were visible from the roadside, thrilling everyone with their breaching antics. Many motorists pulled over, stopping to enjoy a dramatic display as the whales slapped the water with their huge tails. False Bay, rich in marine life, was also home to thousands of seals. Occasionally a great white shark visited the area to snack on a few seals.

Gradually as more people moved in and the cleaning volunteers worked steadily in each room, Wavecrest became less disgusting and more liveable. I began to relax and enjoyed helping others in limbo to feel part of our small community. We all shared what we had and appreciated the privacy that hadn't existed at Surf Inn.

The boys had settled into our new home quicker than I had expected. Eli had turned eleven in July, while Joshua turned seventeen a week after moving to Wavecrest. I was very proud of them for facing enormous challenges in an unfamiliar lifestyle, which seemed to accompany a missions career.

However, two days before Joshua's birthday, he felt despondent. Funds for a party or presents were lacking, and most of his friends were away on outreach. He was lonely. I prayed for God to give me some creative ideas, then invited the Wavecrest residents to celebrate Joshua's birthday with us. My dear friend Elaine, who lived in a flat next to Surf Inn, offered to bake him a cake.

Elaine and I had "clicked" when we first met. I regularly popped in to visit her after she finished work at the hairdressing salon which was situated next to her flat. Sometimes I was so exhausted that I would cry as I told her what I was going through. Knowing anything I said to her was confidential and she would diligently pray for us gave me much-needed comfort. When I spoke about needing to leave Surf Inn, Elaine immediately invited us to live with her. Her generosity and kindness were typical of her compassionate heart. During this phase, I thought of Elaine as my safety net, because I knew she would be there for us if all else failed.

Another reason I enjoyed Elaine's company was because she had a deep longing to participate in missions. Even though her life had often been difficult, she made a joke out of situations that would have made others cry. I valued her kindness and gentleness. Kindness was not always easy to find! Even though I was deeply grateful for Elaine's offer, I knew having my two lads, her two girls, and the two of us would be a squash in her compact three-bedroom flat. I declined her sacrificial invitation and reconciled myself to living at Wavecrest instead.

With guests coming and Elaine providing the birthday cake, I relaxed and trusted God to provide a present for Joshua. Naturally, I was curious how he would do this. On the morning of Joshua's birthday, Eli and I gave him a breakfast of bacon, eggs, and toast and jam in bed. Afterwards, we sang happy birthday. This treat seemed to start the day off nicely. Later, a friend from his youth group rang to say they were arranging a surprise party for him on Friday night. How wonderful! I was relieved that others were also thinking of blessing Joshua. Later in the afternoon when I checked my account at the bank, I was delighted to discover Bev had sent September's support early. Wow, perfect timing. After withdrawing some cash, I hurried off to buy Joshua a present before he returned from school.

At 7 p.m., staff and students began filling up the downstairs room. A resident had decorated the foyer with balloons and streamers, making the place look colourful and festive. Renee from the hospitality department arrived with two milk tarts she had cooked. We had a wonderful evening playing table tennis, singing happy birthday to Joshua, and eating an array of tasty snacks and cakes. Later I lay in bed thinking about all the wonderful blessings from God. He had come through spectacularly for Joshua, making me a happy mother.

A week later, Joshua was asked to lead worship at his youth group meeting, as he played the guitar well and had a tender heart towards God. This was nerve-wracking for him but also an affirmation of being accepted and valued.

Life at Wavecrest sometimes reminded me of scenes from The Sound of Music, where an old, run-down building was transformed into a happy family home. One Saturday night, I made "hokey pokey," a traditional New Zealand candy. Everyone was fascinated by its appearance and taste, as it was their first time sampling the sweet, sticky candy.

Just as I was feeling settled at Wavecrest, I had an unexpected visit from Hugh, who relayed a message from the leadership. After discussing our situation, they felt we needed to return to New Zealand so the boys could finish their education while I raised an adequate support base. I was shocked because when I was filling in the application forms in New Zealand I had gone into great detail about the call on my life. This included the fantastic way God had shown me in a vision that I was destined for Africa and how he had prepared me for ten years before I left New Zealand. There was no doubt in my mind that God had called me to Africa. I don't remember how I responded to their decision about us leaving South Africa, but I knew arguing wouldn't help, so I just listened. After praying for me, Hugh returned home. Even though I knew he was concerned for us, I still felt abandoned and rejected.

Later that night as I lay on my bed, I decided there was no way we were going back home. I said, "God, I am not going. Even if the boys and I have to sleep on the beach, I am not leaving Africa!" How could we anyway? I hadn't bought return tickets, so it wasn't an option for us. But I kept that fact to myself while I quietly pottered around Wavecrest each day.

Soon afterwards, my DTS leaders, Mark and Jenny Kirby, came to visit. They had been on leave at Mark's parents' home after the DTS outreach. After discovering where we lived, they came to assure me of their support. Mark later said they would have invited us to live with them if they had been around when we needed accommodation. Their words of kindness and encouragement during several visits meant a lot to me.

Mark arrived one morning with some tinted paint, a welcome change from ordinary white. I loved the transformation in each room with the coloured pigments. Mine became pink; Sandra's, light purple; and Tom's, blue. Being a patriotic American, he added red, white, and blue striped sheets to his decor!

Slowly the bathrooms were cleaned and repaired, providing hot running water for showers. A donated stove enabled us to cook meals. The appliance I missed most was a washing machine. Without one on the premises, I again tackled all our washing by hand. This task was time-consuming and especially difficult when wringing water out of sheets. My hands weren't strong, so the sheets were still drenched when I hung them outside, making me eager for someone to donate a washing machine!

Even though I was making progress with the appearance and atmosphere in Wavecrest, I knew I was not in a good place with God. He felt remote, and I still felt lost and insecure. I struggled to comprehend why God had allowed so many negative experiences to happen in such a short time. Sadly, these uncertainties had demoralised and robbed me of my usual positivity and confidence. Gone was the sense of peace, connectedness, trust, and safety. In its place were many questions. Had I made a dreadful mistake in coming to Africa? Had I not heard from God? What had seemed so right in New Zealand had since become confusing. I longed for clear direction and confirmation from God. Instead, I felt isolated from Him.

The result was that I retreated into my own world, avoiding contact with base staff as much as possible. I spent my days up a tall ladder cleaning walls and sealing joins below the ceiling to stop pigeon poop from escaping. After the joins dried, I returned to the ladder and began painting each bedroom to bless the new arrivals.

At times I felt forgotten, but God had not forgotten me. After a base worship session, Gerrit, a young Afrikaner man, approached me with a scripture he felt God had prompted him to share from Ruth 2:11-12: "I've been told all about what you have done for your mother-in-law since the death of your husband—how you left your father and mother and your homeland and came to live with a people you did not know before. May the Lord repay you for what you have done. May you be richly rewarded by the Lord, the God of Israel, under whose wings you have come to take refuge."

I began weeping. It was the exact scripture God had highlighted to me in Blenheim in 1981. He used Gerrit to remind me of his promises. It was sad that I had begun viewing God as cold and remote due to the experiences of the past few months. With little sense of being accepted or supported, I had embraced the lie that God was distant and had left me alone during this painful valley time. It was a lie that had steadily damaged my once-strong faith. I was unsure how to fix the damage.

After finding out that my counselling placement had fallen through, and not having enough finance to rent a small flat, I was mystified as to why God had allowed these major disappointments to happen. The verses in Ruth had stated that God would reward me, but instead, moving to the derelict Wavecrest had been freaky and seemed to confirm that struggling for the basics in life was our portion. Feeling shell-shocked and numb, I had stopped reading my Bible or praying for the first time in my Christian life. I had no idea what to say to God, who seemed silent and uninterested in our plight.

Thankfully Sandra, who had also been through a series of disappointments, was in Wavecrest with me. Together, we struggled to make sense of the mess we were in after enthusiastically giving up everything to serve God in missions. Sandra had joined the School of Frontier Missions, intending to head to Russia afterwards. A friend's husband had supported her with R 100 a month during the school, while her mother and family also regularly sent money. Sandra had gradually paid the school fees off but frequently had little spare cash for even a coffee, so she loved to share a meal with me at Mike's Kitchen. Sandra trusted God to provide the air fares and her monthly living costs once she lived in Russia but knew she would have to be intentional in raising adequate support.

At the end of her school, Sandra wrote letters to friends and her church outlining her desire to serve God in

Russia. Sadly, only one person responded with a sizeable amount. It was generous but not enough. Sandra had given up her job and flat when she came to YWAM in January, so she had no choice but to move into Wavecrest with me. We both had a sense of having somehow lost our way; as a result, we became despondent. What were we meant to do now?

Cheska, the base director's wife, visited us; wondering if she was going to tell me that I needed to return to New Zealand, I was instead surprised when she presented Sandra and I with some options for becoming involved on the base. As Sandra had previously worked in an office, she chose to assist Robert Hudson, the registrar at the Cromer Road office. They worked together so well that he told Sandra he was praying she would continue working with him even though he knew Russia, not Muizenberg, was her heart's desire. I was keen to get involved in a project at one of the many impoverished townships nearby, but I was committed to restoring Wavecrest since it was our home, and I was now the manageress!

No matter how confusing life became, God had ways of sending encouraging messages. One day I heard a knock at the front door, and on opening it, I saw Uncle Ron and Aunty May. This wise elderly couple loved people and served the base in a pastoral capacity, often visiting staff needing comfort, advice, or prayer. I knew them slightly from some ministry times during the Counselling School. Aunty May hugged me gently, then asked an unusual question, "Christine, what happens when a heavy tank drives over a little wooden bridge?" Suddenly I realised they understood how I was feeling. "It collapses and gets flattened," I replied.

I stood at the door with this godly couple while unexpected tears ran down my cheeks. After weeks of feeling like an outcast, I was experiencing God's tender heart and a sense of acceptance from them. Only a few words were spoken, but they made a huge impact. Uncle Ron and Aunty May departed after another hug, leaving me feeling nurtured and comforted by their empathetic visit and profound words.

A few weeks later, they visited again with another pearl of wisdom. Aunty May suggested Wavecrest was a life raft for us. "What do you do in a life raft?" she asked me. "You wait to be rescued," I replied. This description of our situation was an "aha" moment. From that point on, I viewed Wavecrest as our battered, old life raft. Its leaks were slowly being sealed, and new passengers were arriving each week. Aunty May encouraged me not to panic but to settle down and trust God while I waited. The life raft analogy was a fantastic picture to hold onto when I felt overwhelmed or confused. I gratefully tucked all the pearls of wisdom deep inside my heart, where they became treasures in a time of darkness.

With Sandra at the office each day and the boys away at school, I spent most days alone. This was a challenge for an extrovert, but I enjoyed watching the progress in our old building. I missed having Rob and Marianne Vermey nearby to talk with. They had moved away from Muizenberg while preparing for their long journey to Malawi. Processing with them had been comforting, as we'd had many similar experiences.

Joshua on outreach bonding with local children.

Chapter 19

Our Life Raft

Life had finally settled into a comfortable routine. Each day after the boys had left for school and Sandra headed off to the registrar's office, I spent several hours up the ladder painting bedrooms. Wavecrest was looking more loved and appreciated after a fresh coat of paint and personal touches by the residents. Rooms were snapped up as fast as I could prepare them, with staff members arriving each week.

Much to my surprise, a project I had reluctantly begun had become a highly satisfying pastime. My natural love of beauty and order determined the quality and imprint of the work I undertook each day.

As a nurturer and extrovert, I thrived among a community of young people. I listened to and encouraged those feeling overwhelmed or unsure about their next steps. Even though the task of cleaning and transforming the old building was daunting, we had some unexpected help. Many of the staff and students on base spent two days cleaning walls, cupboards, toilets, and bathrooms before mopping the floors. Their support was much appreciated as it made a significant difference to the look and hygiene of Wavecrest.

The residents were a diverse group who provided friendship and fun. They each contributed their own unique gifts and sense of connection. Tom from America had a great sense of humour. After watching the movie Fried Green Tomatoes, he encouraged me to watch it too. "You'll love it, Chris. The main character reminds me of you." Naturally, I was keen to see the actress that resembled me, so I bought a ticket. The film was fascinating, with several twists and turns, but I couldn't see why Tom thought I was anything like the young, blonde lead actress.

Back at Surf Inn, I questioned him about his assessment and was flattened by his mystified response. "Not her, Chris. I meant the other lady." Oh, the plump, middle-aged, neglected wife of the selfish, sports-mad husband! But it wasn't the actress's appearance he was referring to. No, it was her spirit and take-charge attitude once she had a plan of action. I secretly chuckled to myself at the mistake. Throughout the movie, I had carefully watched the young, slim blondie, trying to see any mannerism that resembled mine!

One of my favourite residents was Rob, who led the year-long School of Biblical Studies. After knocking an archway through the walls of two adjoining rooms, he created a bedroom and living room. Whenever Rob was home, the soothing sounds of classical music and aroma of freshly brewed coffee wafted around the top floor. His small "apartment" was a magnet to residents wanting to relax, chat, and drink delicious, hot coffee.

Joseph and Mai Banda from Malawi were a wonderful couple on staff who moved into Wavecrest for a few weeks. This short time together allowed us to strengthen our friendship before they headed back to pioneer a new YWAM base in their own country.

Joseph and Mai had endured a lifetime of challenges with patience and fortitude, resulting in rare qualities of humility and surrender. We all appreciated their gentle, loving hearts and profound wisdom. They were a source of comfort and encouragement to us all. I particularly enjoyed their stories about God's goodness and provision. He had faithfully sustained them during all their years in South Africa.

Joshua was thrilled when Ricky, a former youth pastor, moved in. Ricky was a passionate surfer, so they spent many hours on the waves together. I was grateful Josh had someone close by as a sounding board.

This was especially true when Josh arrived home one day saying that his teacher had told him not to return to high school the next year. The reason he gave was that Afrikaans was a compulsory subject Josh had never studied before. No wonder Josh arrived home shocked and perplexed. I was stunned when he relayed this unpleasant news to me and wondered why no one had mentioned this glaring limitation before! However, Joshua's teacher suggested an alternative for 1992, which was to sign up for a course at the local polytech.

This sudden and unexpected change of plans for Josh caught me off guard, so I was grateful he had Ricky to process this with. Ricky was more familiar with the South African education systems than I was. Teen years were challenging at the best of times, but Josh had the additional pressures of living in a foreign country and navigating huge disappointments we hadn't anticipated. Having a close buddy like Ricky to share his problems with made a huge difference in Josh's ability to overcome each new hurdle.

Towards the end of October, my sister Margy wrote telling me that her namesake, Aunty Margy, had died. Because our aunt lived in the same city as my sister, they had developed a close relationship. Margy had become like a daughter to our aunt, who didn't have any children. I hadn't known my aunt well, but just before I left New Zealand, we had spent an afternoon in the city together. I was glad I had prayed with her before we said goodbye; sadly, that was to be the last time I saw Aunty Margy.

A few weeks after receiving the news about my aunt's death, a small parcel containing her watch and wedding band arrived. Margy had been packing up Aunty Margy's home and generously distributing jewellery and furniture among the family. She wanted us all to have a special keepsake.

Around the same time, Bev in Coniston wrote to tell me more people had begun supporting us financially. This was exciting news, as if the increased amount was significant, we would finally be able to rent a flat. Instead of constantly struggling, we would have enough to cover all our needs. I quickly wrote to thank each supporter for their contribution, which was enabling me to train as a missionary in Africa.

For the first nine months, a few faithful friends and family members had kept us afloat financially. I was incredibly grateful to my precious mum, who spun merino wool each day and designed bespoke hand-knitted garments to sell to tourists. These garments truly were a labour of love, as the proceeds from all her hard work (after paying a commission fee) were directed our way. I had trusted God to provide for us and He was faithfully doing that via a variety of people.

Meanwhile in Wavecrest, once we'd got over the shock of our downfall from "missionaries in training" to "impoverished outcasts," Sandra and I had begun praying together. After an honest talk about the lack of prayer in our lives, we decided to meet each morning to worship and pray. We used Sandra's devotional Streams in the Desert as a study guide. I also began to read an Andrew Murray book called *Wait on God*. The title seemed appropriate, as Aunty May had described Wavecrest as a life raft that would provide shelter for us while we waited to be rescued. An encouraging verse Andrew mentioned was "Wait on the Lord; be strong, courageous and never lose hope. Yes, keep on waiting — for the Lord will never disappoint you" (Psalm 27:14). Andrew commented that we needed to be confident and believe God heard us, and that waiting was never in vain.

During our first session together, the Holy Spirit highlighted some heart issues Sandra and I needed to repent of. After that, each morning we felt strengthened by our renewed focus and a strong sense of God's presence. His Word had become our primary source of guidance, insight, and encouragement again. As our faith grew stronger, we gained a different perspective about our situation. We no longer felt alone or adrift, but rather that God had a purpose for our time in Wavecrest. We became more aware that God was with us. He had seen all we had been through and was guiding us even when we didn't realise it.

Understanding God's deep love and involvement in our lives changed how we viewed living at Wavecrest. We now saw the building as God's provision, a place to catch our breath and prepare for the next phase. Also, because of the strong sense of community that quickly developed among the residents, we began to thrive instead of trying to survive. Sandra and I were determined to remain steady and patient while we waited for God to open new doors for us.

Another area God highlighted for me was my fear of failure and sense of not being enough. This negative image often led me into performance and people-pleasing, which were very draining. A book I was reading described Jesus as a humble servant to His disciples. He accepted the tax collector and rough fishermen as they were, while providing the loving support and guidance they needed to mature. Even though some leaders might be rigid and controlling, that was not a true reflection of God's character.

This insight was freeing, as I needed to understand God did not expect perfection—an impossible standard for anyone. The reality was that we would all make mistakes in life, but God would gently correct and keep guiding us.

As if to reinforce the importance of having an accurate picture of God and myself, a guest speaker at a base meeting delivered a short message that contained a surprising punch. She began talking about how we are similar to a tube of toothpaste. The pressures of life had the same effect on us as pressure had on the toothpaste tube. She asked, "What happens when you squeeze a tube of toothpaste?" The answer was simple; what is inside will come out. "Yes," she agreed, "and that's the same as when pressure comes onto our life—what is inside us will come out."

Eek! Over the years, I had generally seen myself as a strong woman of faith. Yet I couldn't deny I had become a critical, distrusting person trying to hide how I felt. The message was so simple that I couldn't avoid the truth, make excuses, or blame anyone. Pressure had revealed the reality of what was in my heart. Having the condition of my soul revealed was heartbreaking, but I knew it was time to repent. This I did with much sorrow and tears. Dear God, how had I allowed so much yuck into my heart? But rather than condemn or reject me, my Heavenly Father opened His loving arms wide to welcome me home, so He could heal and strengthen me.

I was safe with the One who loved me most, but who I had been keeping at a distance.

The message reinforced that, regardless of what anyone did or did not do, we were to stay dependent on God for healing and guidance. As none of us was perfect, we would continually hurt or let each other down in our brokenness and humanity. So there was no valid reason to hide away from or judge one other. Because people repeatedly took offence at each other, Jesus frequently spoke about the need for forgiveness during his time on earth.

As I walked home, I reflected on what I had just heard, acknowledging there was much more to learn than I had realised. This was a sobering thought! Once back in my room, I spent time updating my journal with the new insights that God had shown me that morning.

Consistently writing in my journal had become a habit over many years. I found that writing was a helpful way to process and a safe way to express myself. My journals were full of experiences and lessons learnt as well as key scriptures God used to speak to me. These had all impacted my life significantly, so I wanted to keep a record of my personal journey in case I ever wrote a book about my adventures with God in the future.

While reading the book of Ruth in the Bible, I saw a note I had written some years earlier at the beginning of chapter three: "Naomi realised they would soon become destitute when the harvest finished. Rather than her belief in God's provision making her passive, she used her faith as a springboard for action." Reading this, I felt it was a short but clear message to me about faith and action belonging together.

Even though I was helping with a sewing project for domestic workers in my spare time, I realised I needed something more substantial in the future. However, I had a dilemma; while I was keen to work in a more African setting than a white, middle-class beach town, there was no way I would rock the boys' world again by moving from the Cape.

After emigrating to South Africa, they had faced many challenges, including living in a large YWAM community. I was proud of how they had overcome each obstacle and finally settled into their new environment.

Josh had accepted that he would be studying at the polytechnic next year and was excited about spending several weeks surfing with his buddies during the summer holidays. Plus, he had recently met a lovely girl at his youth group. Being "special" to someone had quickly changed his outlook on life in South Africa!

Eli had matured considerably during the year, becoming a flexible and more responsible young lad. Having a close set of friends and a teacher who regularly affirmed him had a positive impact on him. The following year, 1992, would be Eli's last year of primary school, then in 1993 he would attend Muizenberg High School. Meanwhile, he was no longer ashamed of his unusual home, instead appreciating the social aspect of living at Wavecrest. A key factor was that several residents had taken a special interest in Eli and treated him as a younger brother, which he enjoyed.

Both the lads were settled and optimistic about the coming year. This was a relief for me. The unfavourable event of moving into decrepit old Wavecrest had somehow become a positive experience for us all. I recently read a verse that accurately expressed my journey during the months we spent in the "life raft" (the nickname I gave Wavecrest): "I will never forget what you've taught me, Lord, but when I wander off and lose my way, come after me, for I am your beloved" (Psalm 119:176).

CHAPTER 20

Blessings

Watching gigantic whales from the boys' bay window was a fabulous treat I never tired of. Being so high up, the view of the sea was panoramic. This was one of the many blessings we had discovered since moving into Wavecrest in early September.

From the humble beginnings of my early attempts at fixing and painting bedrooms alone, there was now a small team of us most days. It was a delight to share the responsibility and have fun while working together. During the first weeks, a group of seventy staff and students had spent hours cleaning and doing much-needed repair work at Wavecrest. This made a massive difference to the workload. By the end of November, there were seventeen residents. We had become a close-knit, supportive community that I loved being a part of.

Another positive difference in our life was the increased monthly financial support from New Zealand. This had lifted a burden off me as I was finally able to pay all our expenses on time. The impact for the boys was that their mother was not feeling so stressed, and because money wasn't as tight, they had treats more often! I also enjoyed blessing others who were struggling as we had initially.

Each week I looked forward to two outings. One was to the sewing group on Thursday afternoons, the other was to my church on Sunday mornings. Both outings allowed me to engage with people outside the transitory YWAM world with its constant goodbyes to friends.

Travelling to Wynberg suburb by train on Thursdays was fun. I enjoyed watching people. African people dressed very colourfully compared to my nation, with bright, vibrant dresses and matching head-wraps twisted into fascinating shapes. Each Thursday, I taught sewing to a group of domestic servants (maids) as part of a community development scheme. This activity quickly became the highlight of my week, because I had fun interacting with the ladies. They enjoyed singing while they worked, which was a delight. Their beautiful, harmonious singing filled the room, uplifting us all.

During the last lesson for the year, when I taught the ladies how to make a pair of children's shorts, one of the ladies, Veronica, told me an unbelievable story. She and some other maids felt tied to their elderly "madams," who insisted they work seven days a week. The demanding workload left them with no free time, and as they weren't allowed to invite friends to visit, it became a very lonely lifestyle. Even though they felt stifled and trapped, they were scared to leave their jobs in case they couldn't find another one. Unemployment was very high throughout the nation.

Veronica told us about her last Christmas break when she went home to her family for her annual two-week holiday. At the end of the first week, they were shocked when a policeman knocked on the door and asked for Veronica. He had a message from her elderly madam: "Come back immediately. The temporary helper was not suitable." Veronica longed to stay with her family but knew it would end her employment if she did. She hurriedly packed her suitcase, hugged her husband and teenage children goodbye, then boarded a train to Cape Town. Veronica was not thanked for cutting her time with her family short or even given money to reimburse her train fare.

Other maids shared similar stories of only seeing their own families for a week or two once a year. I could not imagine living like that; it would break my heart to be parted from my sons. Hearing Veronica's story made me grateful for the many freedoms I had taken for granted.

November was a month of many wonderful blessings for us, including something special from Margy. My generous sister had sent an enormous cardboard box full of goodies for me and the boys. After being told it was on its way, we eagerly waited for the box to arrive. Once it arrived in Cape Town, it took us several attempts to submit the paperwork and pay customs clearance fees before we could collect it. Finally, two guys carried it upstairs to my room. Knowing how long the box had been at sea and the rough way it was probably handled at the docks and in storage, I was amazed to see it was still intact.

I longed to rip it open and discover what was inside, but knowing the boys would want to do that, I waited for them to arrive from school. Opening the top, we discovered it was filled with an eclectic mix of goodies that included Aunty Margy's pots and tea towels, a one-hundred-year-old china tea set, toys for the lads, and yummy treats. It was exciting for the three of us to pull out layers of wrapped-up objects. The arrival of such an exciting haul of goodies reminded us that Christmas was not far away. After a hectic year, I looked forward to having time off in December to rest and enjoy the beautiful city of Cape Town with the boys.

Other blessings that came our way were extra money from Mum and Margy plus R 50 from Polly and a box of toiletries from Gerdie's class. Gerdie, the lady who had splattered her chocolate ice cream over some train passengers and herself, had gone back to teaching after her DTS outreach in June.

From time to time, I wondered how Ramona (the little girl I brought home from outreach) was getting on, as she had a special place in my heart. Then one afternoon I had a wonderful surprise when the doorbell rang, and Eli went downstairs to answer it. He called out, "Mum, it's Ramona!" She flew up the stairs and launched herself into my arms, crying and clinging to me. Moments later, a woman appeared with a toddler. It was Ramona's mother, Kathleen, holding Yalzado. I was stunned, as I had been curious about Kathleen but when the father and children moved from the shack, I wasn't sure if I would ever see them again. Naturally, I was thrilled that Ramona's mother had found us.

Kathleen told me her husband wasn't caring for the children properly, so they now lived with her in a women's refuge. It was cramped, as two women and six children shared one bedroom, but Kathleen was hopeful she would be given a council home soon. She had already bought some new furniture with her machinist's wages in anticipation of moving. I rang Michelle to come and see Yalzado, who she had cared for when he was just a baby. Now he was walking. Michelle and I were delighted to be reunited with the children and finally meet their mother.

I made lunch for us all before walking to the marketplace, where I bought Ramona a present for her eighth birthday. She told me she didn't go to school, as her mother needed her to stay home and look after Yalzado while Kathleen was away at work. My heart broke when she described the house mother as a mean lady who slapped her face regularly.

Her situation was far from ideal. Ramona was still vulnerable, with no adult around to protect her. I felt powerless to help her. She cried and clung to me as we walked to the train station, once again pleading with me to let her stay. All I could do was cuddle and comfort her. She needed to leave with her mother. I gave Kathleen money for the train fares and some extra to pay her debt. When she gave me her phone number, I hoped it meant Ramona would become a regular part of our life again.

She looked so vulnerable and sad as we hugged goodbye and they boarded the train. Watching her cry as the train moved away, I prayed for God to protect her. My heart was heavy with the pain of her situation. If we were settled, I would have asked her mother if I could foster her. But realistically, I knew Kathleen wouldn't want to be separated from Ramona again. Also, Kathleen needed her to babysit Yalzado while she was away working. It was an unfair situation for such a bright little girl.

At the end of November, the boys only had two weeks until their school year ended. I knew they eagerly anticipated enjoying hot summer days with friends and an end to classes and homework for several weeks. I, however, was restless as there was not much for me to do at Wavecrest any longer. The season of being manageress was possibly coming to an end. My constant prayer was for an affordable flat to become available soon.

Living somewhere private appealed to me. The doorbell at Wavecrest rang continually due to people visiting the seventeen residents. I also longed for fully functioning appliances like a fridge that we didn't have to share with multiple people, and a reliable stove that worked properly. A lounge where we could entertain our friends would also be nice. The stove at Wavecrest had "shocked" me twice (after being fixed), making me hesitant to use it. And after two and a half months of handwashing all our sheets, towels, and clothes each week, I was ready for a washing machine. My hands were not strong enough to wring out the heavy wet sheets, so I had to find someone to help me each time. The thought of simply putting clothes or linen in a machine and then pressing a few buttons to get the job done was tantalising.

After ten weeks at Wavecrest, something marvellous happened. My kind friend Elaine, the hairdresser, told me she was moving in January and wanted to give me the first opportunity to apply to rent her flat. Her mother had bought a house and invited Elaine and the girls to move in with her. Elaine was excited about moving and knew I had been praying about a place of our own. Her three-bedroom flat was a perfect size, and the rent was affordable. I enthusiastically shared the good news with the boys, who I imagined would be as excited as I was. To my surprise, however, neither of them was desperate to leave Wavecrest.

Knowing we could potentially be living in a place of our own by January, I was keen to look through Elaine's flat and make a list of what we needed to set up our new home. The following week, Elaine showed Eli and me through her home. It was painfully obvious that we needed everything, as the only furniture we had at Wavecrest were some beds on loan from Surf Inn. Elaine stunned me with her sensitivity and generous heart. Having visited us at Wavecrest, she knew our situation. Elaine offered to leave a carpet square and desk for Eli's room, a sewing table in my room, all the drapes and net curtains, and the lounge suite. All she wanted for everything was R 200, the equivalent of NZ$20. Her generosity made me cry.

I trusted God to supply enough finance by January to cover the rent and electricity deposits plus Joshua's polytechnic fees of R 600 and his textbooks. The combined total seemed formidable, but I had peace that it would happen so happily committed to renting Elaine's flat. When I told Mark Kirby I was leaving Wavecrest, he thanked me for all the hard work it had taken to get Wavecrest up and running. It was nice to be appreciated.

The offer of Elaine's flat was the first of several blessings that week. A lady in the community gave me some lovely fashionable clothes, which updated my plain wardrobe. Then I was given two large bags of beautiful material from a lady who had been helping out in her father's fabric shop. On the last day, he gave her offcuts and ends of rolls, which she generously gave to me. I was excited, feeling like a kid in a candy shop as I imagined all the garments I could make.

From an early age, I had made my own clothes and then later the boys' shorts and trousers. I loved looking at and touching fabrics, imagining what I could sew with them. Most of all, it was fun sharing material with others and seeing the joy on their faces as they chose some lovely pieces. One of the residents regularly raised finance by creating colourful garments and bags. She needed something special to make her mum a birthday gift. The timing was perfect.

My heart was full of gratitude to God, who had demonstrated that He cared for both the big and the seemingly insignificant desires of my heart. We had a great deal to look forward to, with the promise of a flat in the New Year. In fact, our summer was looking a whole lot brighter.

Happy summer days.

Eli aged 11.

Chapter 21

Big Changes

Looking back over the previous eleven months, I was grateful for God's constant faithfulness. He had kept us safe, provided for our needs, and guided us day by day as we faced some very tough situations.

The boys' school year was coming to a close. After they sat their final exams, we attended the prize-giving ceremony at Muizenberg Primary School. Eli was excited about the possibility of an award, as he had achieved high marks in most subjects.

I was curious to see how the non-white children had fared, because of the high educational standards. When we arrived, hundreds of parents and family members were milling around, chatting as they found seats.

I watched Eli when his name was called out, first for a maths prize and later for outstanding academic achievement. He confidently strode across the stage both times, not realising he was making history at the school. Several other non-white children also received prizes for academic excellence in science and other subjects.

Eli the prefect!

Their achievements shattered the widely entrenched perception that non-whites were less intelligent or capable. I was sure some parents present were surprised at the outcome.

Events like these helped to change negative perceptions all over the nation. The highlight of our evening was when Eli was chosen as a prefect for 1992. It was an enormous boost for his self-esteem. After the prize-giving, when we were having snacks and drinks, a steady stream of teachers and parents came to enthusiastically congratulate me on Eli's achievements. I was thrilled for him but surprised at how people were responding to me. After all, he had done all the hard work, attended classes every day, and studied all year. As the evening ended, I chuckled as I commented to a friend, "Wow, that was a big fuss. You would think I had just given birth to him!"

Josh ended his year with positive marks and comments from teachers, who were sad to hear he was leaving. Unfortunately, due to not receiving an exemption for Afrikaans, he could not continue at college. Instead, he would begin a marketing and communication course at the polytechnic in January. Meanwhile, he could surf to his heart's content over the summer months. It was gratifying to see both my sons so happy. They had both adapted well to the Cape lifestyle.

My perspective on YWAM, our time in Wavecrest, and my expectations about being a missionary had also changed. While I had been busy renovating Wavecrest, God had worked in different areas of my life. After ten weeks of hard slog, I felt pretty "renovated" myself! In September, I had felt isolated and insecure and avoided people. But by late November, my confident, extroverted self was back.

However, the days were full of emotion. I welcomed returning friends to the base, while farewelling others who had significantly impacted our lives. Mai and Joseph Banda had been a constant source of encouragement, nurturing, and friendship. Before leaving, they invited me to join them sometime in their home country. I could imagine myself working alongside this gentle, wise couple, but not till the boys had finished their education.

The hardest goodbye was to Rob and Marianne Vermey and their children. Rob and Marianne had befriended me in March when they arrived from Holland, supported us financially during my first outreach, provided for our groceries and fuel, then packed our rooms in Surf Inn when I was sick and moved us into Wavecrest. Tears filled my eyes as they squeezed into an old jeep with several other adults to begin the long trek to northern Malawi. Their friendship had made a massive difference to us. I would never forget them.

The next day as I walked home from the shops, I heard someone calling my name. Turning around, I saw a large vehicle approaching, with Josh and Eli's friend Charlie hanging out a window shouting, "Help! We need lunch!" The School of Evangelism students had returned from their extended outreach to debrief and graduate before leaving for the Christmas holidays.

I knew the boys would be excited that Charlie was back, as he was an adventurer who brought laughter and fun into their lives. With the return of the noisy, energetic students, the atmosphere at Surf Inn once again livened up. The team's leader, Francois, and his staff quickly established a relaxed, homely atmosphere that attracted many other students and staff. Everyone enjoyed hanging out and swapping stories over a coffee and a few slices of delicious hot bread covered in peanut butter and jam.

The base had steadily evolved from a lonely place into one of connection and inclusion. This was partly due to staff being encouraged to join small groups so we could bond and develop friendships. I joined Shelby's group. She planned to teach principles from the Lord's prayer, which she said had strengthened her prayer life. This topic fitted in with what Sandra and I were studying. During this time, I developed close relationships with two women on staff whose sons were Eli's classmates. As mothers, we had common interests and concerns that we discussed together. These friendships made a significant difference in making me feel part of the YWAM community.

After a turbulent year, life was looking pretty good for us as a family, even though it was still a mystery what I would be doing in 1992. With the holiday season approaching, I wasn't perturbed about the lack of direction. I was looking forward to lazy days on the beach and outings to the waterfront in Cape Town. Then suddenly, unexpected doors flew open one after the other!

Robert Hudson, the registrar, rang and asked me to visit his office. He informed me that the manageress of Surf Inn had just given two weeks' notice. An Afrikaner couple she knew well had invited her to join a ministry to young people. I was happy for her, as she would be in a family setting instead of the constantly changing population at Surf Inn. I knew this role had been demanding and lonely at times.

Sitting in Robert's office, I wondered why he was telling me this news, until he surprised me by calmly asking if I would consider taking over her position. Apart from having no desire to take on such a complex and demanding role, I was scared at the thought of ordering and catering for almost one hundred people. I thanked him and said no.

However, the unexpected invitation to take on such a responsible role gave me a new sense of value. The narrative had changed dramatically from September, when I had been instructed to return to New Zealand. Ten weeks later, I felt I was seen as an asset to the base. This shift in perspective took a few days to process but left me with increased confidence and a stronger sense of security. It also gave me the boldness to be honest with Robert about how difficult the year had been.

I wasn't sure if my time with YWAM was over, so I wanted to process this with him. He was a friendly guy and was easy to talk to. Robert listened as I told our story and said he was shocked because he'd been unaware of how difficult life had been for us. I asked him not to repeat what I said but to use my experiences to ensure no one else went through what I had.

His reply startled me. "To be honest, Chris, we weren't prepared for you [a single mother with such a strong conviction about working long term in Africa]. And because we weren't prepared, there wasn't enough help or support for you." He explained that international students and staff were now given more information about life at YWAM Muizenberg and supported as they went through culture shock. I appreciated his honesty and felt comforted by his compassion and understanding.

Then during a staff meeting, the base director commented that Wavecrest residents were a relaxed and joyful community. His affirmation was appreciated and made me wonder if this had any bearing on my being asked to run Surf Inn. Nonetheless, it was a daunting task, and I didn't feel confident or capable of taking on this role.

A few days later, I had another surprise when Rodney, a staff member on my DTS, asked me to pray about co-leading a DTS with him in June. My interest was piqued when he said we would run the school in a coloured township, and it would be more practical. His plan was for the students to attend lectures in the morning, then separate into two groups for the afternoon. Rodney would train the boys in mechanics while I taught the girls to sew. As he shared his vision, I became excited. This different set-up was more relational and among a people group I felt at home with.

That night I eagerly wrote to my friends and family about this new venture, which aligned with my skills and vision. But before I even had time for a planning meeting with Rodney, a third invitation came my way. The school leader of the January DTS asked if I would pray about joining his staff. Even though I was amazed at having multiple offers in such a short space of time, I was interested in staffing both DTS's. The timing seemed to dovetail perfectly. I would gain valuable training in the January school that would equip me for working with Rodney in June. Overall, there appeared to be an obvious benefit in staffing them both.

As I sat on some rocks looking out to sea, I replayed the last few days' events. It was surreal how everything seemed to be lining up perfectly. Even though I had felt restless for some time, I was glad I hadn't committed to an office job. To my surprise, God had rewarded my patience with two fascinating opportunities.

When I relayed all the good news to my elderly cheerleaders, Aunty May and Uncle Ron, they were thrilled for me, saying, "We are proud of how you coped during your time at Wavecrest." The waiting was ending, and life was looking a whole lot brighter with a great deal to look forward to in 1992.

CHAPTER 22

Curry for Christmas

"Life is what happens when we are busy making plans" was written on the back of a sugar sachet. I chuckled when I read it, but this little saying was actually a very apt description for December 1991. My plan had been to rest, swim, and spend lazy days sightseeing in Cape Town. Instead, I was asked to help turn Surf Inn into summer holiday accommodation for paying guests. Wow, that was a curveball I hadn't seen coming!

After the YWAM schools had completed their graduation ceremonies and many students had left, I commandeered the remaining students to help carry furniture from Surf Inn to Wavecrest. Fifteen staff and students embarked on the mammoth task of preparing eight flats and thirty rooms for the first holidaymakers, due to arrive on Sunday. Somehow, I had landed the role of directing the flow of furniture from several places into Wavecrest. But I actually enjoyed it as I love organising and bringing order to situations. All day we moved furniture, made up beds, and sorted out cutlery and crockery for each holiday flat.

At about 6 p.m., Eli walked past and said, "I was looking for you, Mum—does supper ring a bell?" Oh my goodness, I had been so busy that I hadn't fed him all day! After rummaging around in the enormous fridges, we heated an array of leftovers. Once we sat down, I realised how exhausted I was. I was grateful to the strong young guys who had dismantled the surplus pine bunk beds and carried them over to Wavecrest. The beds would be stored for six weeks and returned to Surf Inn in time for the January DTS. Meanwhile, the cramped dormitories were transformed into guest accommodation for families, couples, and singles.

The main downstairs room at Wavecrest looked like a cluttered secondhand furniture shop. It was crammed full of beds, side tables, and wardrobes. The YWAM flats along the road were also cleared out before being set up as self-catering family units.

Just when I thought we had finished moving furniture, an elderly lady who ran a coffee shop nearby asked if she could store her personal belongings at Wavecrest. In between sobs, she explained that her stepson had arrived unexpectedly and announced he was taking over the family business. He insisted she move out immediately. The dear lady was shocked and distressed by his callous behaviour. Naturally, I agreed to help. Some students accompanied her to the cafe and returned with several items that we somehow squeezed in between everything else. As I surveyed the crowded downstairs rooms, I felt like we were drowning in furniture.

Then, while we were busy setting up the hotel, I was asked to find accommodation for an extra twelve people. These were staff and students who needed somewhere to sleep for a few nights before returning to their hometowns. To add to this challenge, a Swiss girl arrived a month early for the January DTS and was experiencing jet lag after her long flight. I put her in my room, as nowhere else was available. She slept most of the day. Later that day, a Russian Jewish girl also arrived a month early. I had no choice but to put her into a resident's room who was away for the night. Once they were settled, I headed back to Surf Inn to continue setting up the holiday lets.

Jenny—a friendly, bubbly lady who had volunteered to run Surf Inn as manager for six months—stayed for a few days to help before heading home. She was an upbeat, artistic person and easy to relate to. I looked forward to getting to know her more in 1992 when I would be on the staff of DTS. Jenny was excited about making some changes to the menu and staying with YWAM. Her enthusiasm was contagious.

The following person to arrive was Glynnis, who would be running Surf Inn over summer. Her family accompanied her. Glynnis appreciated our help and shared her plans, asking if I would be the cook, as breakfast was included in the tariff. Cooking breakfast in a hotel would be a new experience, but I agreed. Glynnis wanted to redecorate the tired, well-used dining room, so we painted and wallpapered till almost midnight.

It was satisfying working with Glynnis because she was a creative lady with some great ideas. After cutting out laminated floral tablecloths, the room looked cheery and smart. Each guest room was given a final clean after the beds were made up with matching duvet covers. It was just as well we worked fast because guests arrived days earlier than anticipated!

Most days, Glynnis and I worked hard for twelve to fourteen hours. We moved between buildings, ran upstairs and down, and checked everything was ready. Each morning I cooked breakfast, then made new pillow slips. After all the preparations were complete, I took some time to write overdue letters to my family. I knew they would be wondering how we were spending our

Christmas holidays and could imagine their surprise when they discovered I was helping to run a hotel.

The first week we had some demanding guests from Johannesburg who were hard to satisfy. Thankfully I had relined the shelves in their kitchenette and ironed the freshly laundered drapes. We replaced an older toaster with a new one, and because they were Jews, I asked Janna, the young Russian Jewish lady, if she would cook for them. After finding a room for Janna at Wavecrest, I spent time getting to know her story.

Earlier in the year Janna and her brother were allowed to leave Russia to visit Israel, then a church group sponsored her to attend a YWAM Discipleship School. She chose the Muizenberg school. Sitting together, we used Janna's Russian–English dictionary to explain words like pepper, beetroot, and milk. "Aha," she would say when she found the Russian word for each item. I enjoyed the novelty of having Janna as a friend, especially as I had never expected to meet a Russian in Africa!

As more guests arrived, Josh landed a job cleaning two flats each morning. Working for Glynnis gave him some pocket money for the holidays. After a few days, I noticed he was reluctant to clean a particular flat, until I remembered two teenage girls were staying there. Naturally, Josh felt embarrassed vacuuming and cleaning the flat while the girls hung around and watched him work. He was a good-looking lad who had attracted their attention. I went with him and entered first, then encouraged the girls to visit the beach while he got on with his job. After his cleaning stint each day, he was free to join his mates on the beach or explore Cape Town with Charlie and others.

Eli also earned some pocket money with an enterprise he started after an Indian guest enquired whether anyone could vacuum his car. Eli offered to vacuum and clean his car for R 5. The guest promptly drove his BMW to the parking area near Surf Inn, where Eli took great pains to give it a thorough clean. Supportive Charlie made an appointment sheet on A4 paper and pinned it to the hotel noticeboard. I didn't know if there would be a great demand, but it helped Eli feel part of the holiday hotel, and he earned enough cash for ice creams and rides on the Supertubes hydro slide. In contrast, Josh planned to buy clothes with the money he earned. We had become an enterprising family overnight!

Glynnis suggested I opened a coffee shop in the evenings, using the dining room. She said I could keep the profits, so I had a sign made and opened "The Kiwi Coffee Shop" with some cakes made by a friend. Music by Kenny G created a mellow ambience. I didn't make much profit, but it was fun to have friends drop by for a chat and to sample the yummy cakes.

Just as we thought everything was settled and running well, a guest complained that their double bed was on a lean. Two students hauled the offending bed over to Wavecrest, where we swapped it for my one. That night, trying to sleep on the leaning bed, I knew mine would be an improvement for our guests!

Meanwhile, as I prayed about what potentially lay ahead, I hoped it would include travelling around Africa. However, without any specific details, I needed to tuck this longing away and focus on being a mum to my wonderful, enterprising sons. I was content to stay put while they completed their education. Watching them mature and become more confident during the year had been very rewarding.

As the days were quite hot, I developed a habit of waking at 6 a.m. and walking along the beach. It was a great way to start my day—except when it was windy. Walking back to Wavecrest at the end of a long day, I marvelled at how much we had achieved. The old building was still rundown in some respects, but I had gained pleasure watching each room become fresh and lovely as we painted walls and hung curtains. Also, I had been able to run Wavecrest like my own home, which resulted in a relaxed, caring community.

Being away from a strict, inflexible environment was liberating and had brought healing for myself and others. There were fewer rules, with a stronger focus on relationships. I was thrilled at how quickly we all bonded. Sharing our resources, eating, praying, and laughing together created a wonderful family atmosphere.

A surprising aspect of being a foreigner in a nation steeped in segregation and prejudice was how openly non-white students spoke to me. They felt safe enough to talk honestly. Pamela, a young lass from Namibia, shared how difficult it was being a coloured person in a white community. She saw things from a different angle, but being in the minority, she was hesitant to speak out. Unfortunately, Pamela had been repeatedly hurt by the unconscious slights of other students. Being raised in an apartheid system, the students had spent their lives relating to coloured people as inferior—mainly only as their domestic servants. I listened and prayed with her, as I was well aware of how deeply ingrained prejudice and division was in South African society.

Unfortunately, the average South African had been brainwashed by the government into believing the different groups had varying levels of intelligence. For example, a lady from my church had startled a coloured lady and myself while we were travelling in her car by stating, "Of course, we can't intermarry because coloureds and blacks have different genes than whites." I turned to the lady sitting in the back seat beside me to see her reaction. She had just discovered she supposedly had inferior genes to our driver. We both raised our eyebrows at this shocking statement. All we could do was pray for our friend's beliefs to change.

I was staggered that intelligent, kind Christians could believe such absolute nonsense. Another common misconception was about the huge difference in living standards. Many black Africans experienced extreme hardship, but if we referred to this, locals often became tense and touchy, saying, "They are used to it and quite happy with their lives." I knew I presented a challenge to my South African friends because I was obviously not devoid of intelligence, yet I had dated and loved a black man. This was absolutely unthinkable to most of my new friends — even appalling to some.

Learning to bridge these enormous chasms of worldview was a challenge that remained for many years. Meanwhile, I learnt to appreciate other qualities in each person and knew that it would take a revelation from God to shift their thinking and understanding.

Our first Christmas in our new country was only days away when an Indian family staying at the hotel offered to make Christmas lunch for everyone. I was intrigued to see what was on the menu and relieved someone else would be cooking. Our Indian guests were friendly people from Durban, another famous surfing spot.

After the breakfast clean-up, I handed the kitchen over to them and eagerly awaited our surprise lunch. Glynnis and I set the tables, then called everyone to join us. We were served an authentic Durban curry for Christmas lunch by our Hindu guests. It was delicious, spicy, and a great way to celebrate together.

The following two weeks flew past, then it was time to dismantle the guest hotel and move all the furniture back from Wavecrest to Surf Inn. Once the dormitories and rooms were set up, I felt physically and mentally exhausted. Thankfully there was a two-week break before the new Discipleship Training School started, so I had some time to rest before lectures began. I looked forward to working with Francois and his team. Both the boys and I had new seasons ahead of us in 1992.

Comparing our life to the one we had in Coniston, I was grateful to God that He had given me the courage to sell our home and buy one-way tickets to South Africa. While it had been overwhelming, scary, and lonely at times, we had become more resilient and adaptable. I loved watching the boys grow as they embraced their new lifestyle and thrived among the YWAM community. God had been faithful in every way. I knew He was preparing me for more adventures with Him, which was exhilarating. I would keep saying yes in the years ahead and see what He unfolded.

Even though I was well aware of all the tensions, hardships, and injustices around us, I had learnt that trying to insist people changed their perceptions only led to defensiveness and anger. Instead, I stayed true to my beliefs of everyone being of equal value to God and prayed for the locals to have their own revelation from God. This would radically reframe their belief systems. The truth was that segregation had robbed everyone of an opportunity to develop healthy relationships with people from different cultures. Meanwhile, I was like a kid in a candy shop, surrounded by people from over thirty countries. This was a dream come true.

If 1991 was anything to go by, 1992 would be full of new challenges and unexpected experiences. I felt very fortunate to be living such a dynamic life. When I challenged God in 1980 to "prove" Himself to me, I never dreamt He would lead us to Africa and provide for all our needs, just as He had done for Abraham and Moses. I had read the stories for years, but now we had experienced it ourselves. Naturally, I was keen to see what else He had in store for us.

THE END

What Happened Next?

Christine and the boys

Joshua stayed in South Africa until he was twenty-one. He worked for a German mechanic who saw his computer ability and encouraged him to gain qualifications in that area. After a two-year course in Cape Town, Joshua moved to New Zealand then Sydney. He married and built a career in IT. Josh and his family now live in Christchurch near Eli's family and Christine.

Charlotte, Kaleb (3), Elisha (9), Joshua.

Eli finished his secondary education and then completed a Microsoft certification by self study. Following that, he headed for Sydney and lived with Joshua while working in IT.

Raphael (8), Eli, Naniso (3½),
and Vimbayi.

After returning to YWAM in South Africa, Eli lived with me. He met his lovely wife Vimbayi at YWAM and they married in 2005. They have lived in Christchurch for seventeen years and are raising two children.

270

Christine: I worked with YWAM for most of my twenty-four years in Africa—sixteen years in South Africa and then eight years in Zimbabwe.

In 2012 I returned to New Zealand for seven months when advanced ovarian cancer was discovered. The oncology specialists gave me about ten days to live. After chemo and a long operation, I flew back to Zimbabwe, where the economy was collapsing. I grappled with running a home and a guest house during the days of electricity and water cuts. We navigated the hyper-inflation era where our bank notes reached 100 trillion dollars—the highest inflation in history.

I moved back to New Zealand in 2013. Life had become too complex in Zimbabwe, and my main focus became my health and family. Amazingly enough, Eli, Josh, their families, and I all live within a five-minute drive. We are thoroughly enjoying being able to celebrate birthdays and other special days together. After many years of living on three different continents, we all moved back to Christchurch from 2005 to 2013. Being together again is God's gift to us.

After twenty-four years as a missionary in Africa, followed by seven years recovering from cancer and enjoying my grandchildren, I have a new assignment. My latest assignment is to TELL, writing all the incredible stories about God's provision, protection, and guidance during my twenty-four years as a missionary. During these years, I travelled extensively around Africa, teaching community development seminars to pastors and community leaders.

Because I travelled alone and often only had airfares for the trip to a nation, I repeatedly relied on God to get me back to South Africa. The different methods and people He used to accomplish this were incredible and fascinating. I learnt to "let go and let God" provide as He guided me for two decades in Madagascar, Nigeria, Egypt, Uganda, and other nations. These true events form the basis of this Courage series.

Book three covers 1992 when I was on staff for a Discipleship School and accepted the role of manageress of Surf Inn. I worked with a small, dedicated team to create a warm, caring atmosphere. Being manageress was a huge responsibility but a fulfilling experience that God used to stretch and shape me.

In February 1992, we had a powerful visitation by Holy Spirit at Surf Inn during our DTS. It lasted for three days and three nights. During this time, many students and staff were consumed by waves of God's love, to the extent that we lay on the floor for hours while "electricity like waves" flowed through us. The result was deep healing in many areas of our lives and restoration of our first love and passion to follow Jesus. Soon after this hard-to-explain visitation, we read about the Toronto move of God, which sounded similar to what we had experienced.

Later that year, I took boxes of food to a struggling Zimbabwean base, as the nation was experiencing a prolonged drought. The ways God provided for the trip there and back were eye-opening and the start of many similar journeys throughout Africa. Each time He nudged me to go somewhere else, I simply moved in that direction and watched what unfolded.

I discovered that God is entirely faithful and enjoys us having adventures with Him! Our childlike faith delights His heart.

****

If, like me, you are curious to know what happened to the main characters of stories, read on! However, if this doesn't interest you, skip this section.

Mark and Jenny Kirby: my DTS leaders

After the DTS graduation, Mark and Jenny stayed with Mark's parents for two months to rest and prepare for the next school. However, this didn't eventuate, as new staff members arrived and led the 1992 DTS. Mark and Jenny helped on the base until 1995 when Mark had back surgery for an old injury. It was a scary time, as specialists told him that he could lose the use of his legs. Thankfully he didn't, but it took him six months to recover. Later God spoke to Mark about starting a business, and his YWAM days came to an end.

Meanwhile, Jenny worked in the finance office until 2003. The Kirbys had three children. Unfortunately, the youngest child died from a rare genetic disease at the age of eleven. Their two surviving children still live in South Africa with their families. During a chat last year, Mark and I shared about our experiences in 1991. It was great to speak blessings and pray over each other, having gained a deeper understanding of what we'd encountered.

The Kirbys, who now have two grandchildren, have opened their home to people of different cultures who need the security and safety of a nurturing family. This is a perfect role for such a kind, generous couple.

Anthony and Hanna from Ghana

In 1992 Anthony and Hanna moved to the Transkei region, where Anthony trained as an electrician with Eskom. A regular income enabled them to remain in

South Africa while following God's call on their lives. In Transkei, they assisted a pastor in establishing a church and eventually gained permanent residence.

Anthony and Hanna relocated to East London in 2000, where they established their first church, Victory Life Evangelical Temple, in 2004. Meanwhile, Anthony worked full-time, reaching management level. He resigned in 2009 after seventeen years with Eskom and established his own company to support the church and various ministry projects.

By 2021 Anthony and Hanna had three churches and had trained and ordained eight pastors.

When I spoke with Anthony, they had recently bought buses for each church to help with transport needs and short local community outreaches. Hanna assists Anthony in the various ministries. In addition, she is an international trader who travels to China and London regularly to purchase women's wear.

They continue to be an inspirational couple who refuse to be defined by their ethnicity alone. Their character, dignity, and integrity continue to open doors as they navigate the multi-cultural world of South Africa. From humble beginnings in 1991, Anthony and Hanna continue to impact and transform communities within South Africa. Well done, my precious friends!

The Vermey family

At the end of 1991, Rob purchased a 50-year-old Land Rover with a top speed of 70 km/h to take a mission team of seven adults and three children to Malawi. The journey was painfully slow and uncomfortable, as everyone was cramped. At the Zimbabwean border, they were forced to take a long detour, as anyone with a South African passport was refused entry. To make matters worse, the old Land Rover repeatedly broke down, causing further delays. It was fortunate that Rob was a mechanic!

The old jeep.

Once in Malawi, the team rented a house and began working with a Baptist church. The only available food in the market was onions, tomatoes, cucumbers, beans, and dried fish, which became their daily diet.

The original outreach plan was to stay for two years. However, this changed in the third month when the team received some shocking news from the local visa office. Their visas were denied, and they were told to leave the country immediately. Feeling overwhelmed and dismayed at this unexpected news, everyone packed their belongings, wondering what to do next.

Three people decided to return to their home country, but the Vermeys headed back to South Africa. Rob and others went by jeep, while Marianne and the children were flown out by Air Mission. After a few months, the Vermeys returned to Holland to raise support. Finances had been an ongoing struggle.

Because their church board didn't support missionaries on furlough, Rob worked as a tractor driver on a farm. While helping a man whose truck was stuck, Rob shared his faith and calling. As a result, the man supported them for two years with a substantial amount each month. It felt like a miracle from God.

Marianne discovered a strange perception towards missionaries: at home in your own country, you are the poor missionary, but in many parts of Africa, you're the rich foreigner. "In Holland," she observed, "if I've got one pair of shoes, I am poor. In Africa, a pair of shoes can mean I'm rich."

Overall, it was hard to come to terms with the different world views. After sharing with friends how much they depended on regular support, Rob and Marianne returned to Africa with a more stable financial base. They had moved twenty-nine times since selling their home.

In 1994 Rob and Marianne set up an outreach base in Maseru, a border town in Lesotho, a tiny kingdom within South Africa. They hosted teams who came to work in the rural areas. To their delight, God provided a lovely spacious house for them, where they lived for seven years without any rent increase. Each day the children crossed the border from Maseru into South Africa to attend school. During holiday breaks, the family was able to stay in a luxurious home with a maid and swimming pool while the owners went on holiday.

In 2000 their eldest daughter, Judith, returned to Holland. After many years in Africa, Holland had become a foreign culture to her. With no internet in Maseru, it was difficult for the family to keep in touch. In 2001 Rob and Marianne moved back to Holland with the younger children for some family time.

Their next assignment was to be part of an adult education programme in a refugee camp in Ethiopia. Judith and Christian stayed in Holland to attend university, while Marcia was placed in an international boarding school in Addis Ababa, Ethiopia's capital city. Her school was 750 kilometres away from her parents.

Ethiopia is an impoverished nation, so living conditions at the refugee camp were very basic. There was no electricity, running water, or internet. Once a week, Rob and Marianne drove for an hour to reach an internet outlet so they could stay in touch with the older children in Holland. To spend time with Marcia, they needed to drive to

Addis Ababa every eight weeks. Due to the state of the roads, the journey took them two days. This mission's assignment was painful for the family, who all suffered from being in different countries and locations. Marianne became ill several times, developing rashes all over her body and dropping in weight to fifty kilograms.

After a year in Ethiopia, war broke out. A convoy of Ethiopian aid workers was killed, so all aid workers and missionaries were instructed to leave immediately. Rob and Marianne hurriedly packed a few precious items includ-

Rob, Marianne, Christian, Marcia, and Judith.

ing family photos and then began a hair-raising three-hour journey through the violent areas.

It was eight hours before they could radio their family and mission leaders to say they were safe. Naturally, this was a traumatic time for the children and family back in Holland, not knowing if Rob and Marianne had been hurt or had miraculously escaped.

Marcia, who was in a safer area, waited for news at her boarding school. When Rob and Marianne reached

Addis Ababa, they rented a house for six months while Marcia finished her school year. After that, they decided to return to Holland to reunite and bring stability to the children. The family was once again their top priority.

Finding themselves without any income, Marianne worked as a receptionist and Rob as a bus driver. Unfortunately, their church cut their financial support, not understanding how traumatised everyone was and how they all needed ongoing emotional and financial support while they healed from the trauma and repercussions of the family being separated.

One year later, they began working with a church in Rotterdam. The pastor had a mission heart, focusing on refugees in the city. Rob biked around befriending them. He was in his element.

Then in 2005 something shocking happened. While Rob was out running, he collapsed and died. Unfortunately, because he didn't have any ID in his pockets, Marianne was only informed eighteen hours later. Her life changed in an instant. She couldn't understand how this tragedy had happened when Rob was still young.

Despite battling shock and grief, Marianne continued to work as a receptionist but needed more income. Her church arranged for her to continue Rob's ministry with the refugees. The pay helped for a short time but having two jobs became stressful and gave her no time to grieve the enormous loss of Rob. Finally, after five months, it all became too much, and Marianne broke down. After a much-needed break, she began studying and working again.

Marianne and family.

From 2009 to 2013 Marianne worked twenty-two hours a week as a pastoral worker for her church, then attended college on Fridays. She spent each weekend studying and obtained a theology degree after four intensive years.

Later Marianne met and married a widower called Rene, an IT worker in a bank. In 2018 they moved to Hungary to begin a ministry for widows and widowers. Their vision was to create a warm, homely atmosphere where these older single people could enjoy outings and companionship.

Marianne and Rene bought two adjoining homes, one for themselves, and one to host the groups. They renovate both houses in between the groups staying. Marianne teaches relationship skills with God, self, and others, and prays with those wanting counsel and healing. Every eight weeks, Rene and Marianne

Rene and Marianne Unkel-Mons.

return to Holland for a two-week break with their children and eleven grandchildren.

In 2021 I reconnected with Marianne via Messenger video. It was wonderful to see each other again and discover how our families were doing. She showed me the placard I had given them in December 1991 (with the promises from Psalm 84) on her bedroom wall in Hungary. Because the placard had become old and worn out over the years, a friend had copied the verses out and included the decorative artwork. The placard was placed on a wall in each new home as they travelled around Africa, Holland, and finally Hungary.

I honour my dear friends who made a significant difference in my life in 1991 and served God sacrificially for many years in various mission fields. Life was not easy for the children, with so many moves and being separated from their parents at different times. However, they remain a close family, enjoying regular times together with the added joy of grandchildren.

Sandra Butler

Once Sandra realised that she didn't have enough finances to consider moving to Russia, she offered to return the support money to the generous couple who had gifted it, but they declined to take it back. God had prompted them to support Sandra, and they wanted to obey. They later told her that if she had let them know she needed more money, they would have gladly given the required amount. God has unique ways of closing doors as we try to move ahead.

During this perplexing season, a lady in YWAM saw a scene with Sandra in it while praying. Sandra was standing by the side of the road with her suitcases. Each time a vehicle came by, she enthusiastically picked her cases up, expecting the driver to stop and give her a lift. However, none of them did. Finally, a slow donkey cart came by and stopped beside Sandra. This was the transport God had chosen for her. Through this word picture, Sandra felt God was telling her not to be discouraged because nothing she had expected had come to pass. The vehicles that didn't stop for her were not the right ones. Instead of a fast car, God was sending a donkey cart. The process was going to be slower than she had expected!

Sandra and Karel-Jan.

After the door to Russia closed, the direction of Sandra's life changed completely. She met and married a wonderful Dutch man, Karel-Jan. I attended their beautiful, creative wedding. To Sandra's amazement, when Karel-Jan bought a second-hand car, he unexpectedly called it Donkey! She was amused by this unique fulfilment of God's word to her.

Ironically, Sandra stayed in Muizenberg for several years while Robert Hudson and his family moved to Uzbekistan in 1994 to serve God there. Sandra chuckled when she commented to me recently, "Robert Hudson went to Russia in my place!"

Karel-Jan and Sandra now live in Holland with their teenage daughter, Lailah.

Sandra, Karel-Jan, and Lailah.

Lailah.

Robert and Trudie Hudson

After finishing their DTS in 1990, Robert set up the registrar's office and served there for several years while Trudie continued working the night shift as a nurse. During 1992–1993, Robert promoted YWAM in churches and youth groups to recruit mission-hearted people.

God began challenging Robert about his lack of mission experience, so he led a team of ten people to Uzbekistan in 1994. Having attended a School of Church Planting, Robert had the insight and skills to plant a new church and minister to locals. After two years, the team left, while Robert and Trudie remained for thirteen years. Their sons completed their education in South Africa but flew to Uzbekistan each December for family holidays.

Trudie and Robert have since lived and worked in Hong Kong for thirteen years. They are both involved in the educational field. Trudie has a master's degree in teaching, while Robert teaches English to non-English speaking students.

Their adult children live in the United States, New Zealand, and Hong Kong.

Ida Tobiassen

Ida from Norway enjoyed her time in YWAM, especially the exuberant African style of worship that included passionate singing and energetic dancing. The sense of joy and freedom was a new experience for her, as she came from a conservative Lutheran background and a "quieter" nation.

In October and November of 1991, Ida, Roberto (Italian), and Holger (German) did their practical outreach phase together at Myanmar Mission in Natal. The mission specialised in helping alcoholics. The three students attended counselling sessions involving the alcoholic residents and distributed clothes and food to those in need. In addition, Ida used her creativity to decorate rooms with her artwork and taught Bible stories using simple drawings while a Zulu-speaking man translated for her.

Ida felt held back when interacting with others because English was her second language. However, despite cultural and language barriers, she experienced deep fellowship and friendship through the music. New friends taught her Zulu and Xhosa songs that she still enjoys singing. Ida was curious about life in the "new" South Africa. She wondered what the locals thought about the changing laws, the end of apartheid and segregation, and democracy for all.

It was fascinating discovering what the South African students at YWAM felt about developing friendships across the racial and cultural lines. During her first days, some white students commented that they were tired of boycotts and foreigners voicing their opinions. They felt the world misunderstood the government and apartheid system of South Africa. Ida was reluctant to ask questions directly or give her opinion, so instead, she learnt by observing people.

Ida was young and independent. In Natal, some people were sceptical about her travelling alone, saying it was dangerous. But local Norwegian missionaries told her not to be afraid, so she confidently used the local bus services.

Ida gained a new perspective on her lifestyle. In Norway, she didn't own a house or a car and had to work hard for three years to save money for her trip to

South Africa. After her outreach, Ida returned home with empty pockets to a wealthy country, but she felt rich compared to many of the poor she saw and worked with in Africa.

Back home in Norway, Ida studied childcare for three years in Oslo before qualifying as a social worker. She then worked with children in psychiatric wards and foster care for several years. Ida married Torbjoern Sundsdal in 2004. They live in the countryside of southern Norway, where they serve God in their local church. Ida presently works in a kinder-

Ida with hubby, Torbjoern Sundsal.

garten. Her heart's desire is for the churches and communities to be inclusive, cross-cultural, and Christ-like.

Elaine

At the end of 1991, after giving us most of her furniture and drapes, my dear friend lived with her mother for a short time before moving into her own flat again. Once again, God provided for all her needs.

Today Elaine lives in a suburb of Cape Town. Her adult children live in South Africa, the United States, and Ireland. She has seven grandchildren.

We stay in touch via WhatsApp. I enjoy her zany sense of humour, which shines through regardless of the daily hurdles she faces with her health.

Elaine's trust and dependence on God remains as strong as ever.

FOOTNOTE: If you missed out on book one, *Journey to Courage,* I encourage you to purchase a copy. The link is at www.courageseries.com. Book one tells the story of my life before becoming a Christian then preparing for ten years before I sold my home and flew to South Africa with the boys in 1991.

****

It is late September 2022 and I have just completed book two, *Courage in the Cape.* I am giving myself a few weeks' holiday to watch movies, catch up over a cuppa with friends, and spring-clean the house before starting to write book three.

I am writing eight books to complete the Courage series, covering my early life and twenty-four years in Africa. Make a note of the website, and check periodically to see if a new book has been published. Thank you so much for supporting me as I TELL the stories of God's faithfulness and goodness to us for over forty years!

2021 – selling my first book.

Acknowledgements

Once again, I am grateful to everyone who contributed to bringing this second book in the Courage Series to fruition. Two down, six more to go!

Firstly I want to thank my sons and their families for their endless patience as I shared each part of the writing and publishing journey with them. I know it became repetitive! Your encouragement and patience was appreciated!

To my buddies at Dundee Place where I live: Greg, Kent, Adelie, Glenda, Norm, Yazz, Catherine, Amanda, Anne-Marie, and Marie. Your enthusiasm for my books spurs me on.

To my Wahine Toa buddies for your love and support as I have begun embracing my identity as an author and a storyteller.

To Collette for opening your home and providing me with a lovely, quiet place to write.

To all my friends from 1991 who contributed to this story and added some incidents I had forgotten!

To my proofreaders: Kay Solomon, Laura Spargo, Margaret Francis, and Pearl McNeil. Your eye for detail and suggestions sharpened the storyline.

To my Kiwi editor Susanna Schollum: You made a tedious task relaxing and fun and turned the first draft into something that flowed well. You are a talented lady: editing, laying out the text, inserting photos, and even writing the blurb for the back cover! A big thanks.

To your daughter Nina for helping me find the best way to reproduce old photos for the book.

To Carmen Lye once again for a brilliant cover. Your graphic skills are impressive.

To my buddy Sue Deacon, who has taken me on frequent outings to help me unwind and catch my breath when I was feeling overwhelmed. Thank you for your fantastic company and many mochas!

And finally, to God for His guidance and enabling as I began the all-encompassing journey of writing the sequel to *Journey to Courage*—always so much to learn each time. I needed His help as I endeavoured to capture the essence of our first year in Africa. It was an unexpected start to a 24-year career in Africa. I truly was naïve when I took the boys and left New Zealand.

God's love changed me from an insecure, anxious person into a strong woman of faith and courage. I love telling people about God's goodness, especially now when the world has changed so rapidly and left many people feeling anxious and adrift.

After my experience with cancer in 2021, I am grateful every morning for a new day to spend with my precious family and friends.

Sources

"A Brief History of Durban's Sugar Cane" by Shubnum Khan, August 19, 2017. www.theculturetrip.com

Apartheid education: *Aims of education in South Africa* by Walter Eugene Morrow, 1990

History of ANC: Brittanica

Inside Out by Dr Larry Crabb

Racial classification: BBC News

South African history: www.ducksters.com

The Pass Laws: www.revision.co.zw

Who was Nelson Mandela? By Pam Pollock & Mel Belviso, 2014

Contact

If this book has impacted or inspired you, please email Christine as she would love to hear from you:

Email: Chris@teamnathan.co

f Christine Nathan Courage Series

Website: www.courageseries.com

Christine's Video Testimony:

▶ Youtube/Fantail studios/Learning to live by Trust and Faith